Buying and Restoring Old Property in France

David Everett is the author of *Home Boat Completion* and the *Manual of Pottery and Porcelain Restoration*, also published by Hale. He lives in Southern France.

D1435662

Buying and Restoring Old Property in France

DAVID EVERETT

ROBERT HALE · LONDON

© *David Everett 1992*
First published in Great Britain 1992
First paperback edition 1995
Second paperback edition 1999

ISBN 0 7090 6504 3

Robert Hale Limited
Clerkenwell House
Clerkenwell Green
London EC1R 0HT

2 4 6 8 10 9 7 5 3

Typeset by
Derek Doyle and Associates, Mold.
Printed in Great Britain by
St Edmundsbury Press Limited, Bury St Edmunds
and bound by
WBC Book Manufacturers Limited, Bridgend

Contents

Illustrations

To Ann, my wife and morale RSJ

Introduction

Whilst not setting out to sell France, it might be an idea to point out some of the benefits to those who may be undecided. A brief summary of these would be the cost, climate, cuisine and convenience.

At the time of writing, France represents good value for money, with regard to property. There are probably many reasons both historical and political, but one of the main ones will be the geographical fact that France is about twice the area of the UK with a population slightly less; thus with twice the land per head the natural law of supply and demand has not really begun to make itself felt. Inevitably it will eventually do so though, so property bought now can be expected to increase steadily over the years.

The climate just across the channel is very little different to the south coast of England, but the south Biscay coast and the Mediterranean are a lot warmer with longer summers and shorter winters. A good part of the interior also tends to be warmer by virtue of being further south.

The French cuisine is world famous already and has the added bonus of being very good value. It is cheaper to eat and drink well at restaurants here than in the UK. Shopping for food in the supermarkets is about the same overall. Meat is more expensive but of good quality, and wine is much cheaper. Swings and roundabouts.

France is convenient in many ways: a short sea crossing from the UK with a wide choice of routes, and with the opening of the 'Chunnel' it is now feasible to commute to London from a home near the French end in about the same time as it might take from the West Country. Add to this the fact that your home will have cost less than half of its UK equivalent and one begins to see how the quality of life could be improved. As a result, property in that region is increasing in price at a faster rate than elsewhere, but still represents very good value in comparison. The rush to buy property is now starting, and there is even a unique 'English' village being built in the region of Calais to encourage the already growing trend.

Another convenience is the language which is and always has been the second language in UK schools, giving many people at least a basic knowledge or better. Even those who try hard to communicate with a pocket dictionary and sign language will quickly make friends with the locals who would much prefer you to speak bad French than English at an increased volume. Fortunately, as the French education system is quite efficient, many professional people such as doctors, lawyers, dentists etc., speak our language very well, or at least well enough to come to our rescue when we flounder.

Hobbies, sports and pastimes are pursued with enthusiasm here. There are good libraries and other facilities practically everywhere plus winter sport and summer sailing second to none. For the benefit of those who intend to keep boats here, a recent survey in a leading UK sailing magazine showed marina prices to be, in some cases, as little as a quarter of those on the UK side.

Whether the plan is to buy property for holidays or as a permanent residence, the attractions are many and varied.

I would like to thank Louis Chatoux, chief architect of the Service d'Urbanisme at Agde, and also Chantal Parpaillon, Architect D.E.S.A. and Serge le Couteur, Architect D.P.L.G., both practising in Agde, for supplying me with information.

For ease of reference costs have been calculated on the basis of 10 francs to the pound.

1   What, Where and How to Buy

Unless your budget is limitless, buying any property is a major investment, so careful thought and evaluation is of the utmost importance. Thus it will be as well to consider what, where and how before taking the plunge.

What to Buy
Generally speaking, available old property, which is what this book is about, can be divided into three types: those that are in a town or village centre (mostly terraced cottages, houses and apartments), farms and outbuildings – including barns – and large country chateaux.

Historically, apart from farmers and landowners, the bulk of the population has stayed within the bounds of the town or village. Detached or semi-detached property on the outskirts of towns are a fairly recent phenomenon, but the trend to move further out is continuing, leaving a lot of traditional urban dwellings available for sale and ripe for development. A lot of these will be in very narrow streets and clustered around the church or cathedral which was once the hub of the old quarter. It is not unusual here for owners to be able to open their shutters and have a conversation or, in extreme cases, even shake hands with the opposite neighbour a scant few feet away. Frequently they were built back to back, denying the possibility of opening up windows at the rear, thus needing other methods, to be discussed later, to make them attractive living places. Gardens are more common in the villages towards the north, but elsewhere they are rare in the town or village centre, although a few properties are blessed with an enclosed courtyard. This makes some unworthy of renovation, but a careful search will reveal many exceptions. Obviously corner sites have the advantage of more windows, and south facing positions will let in more light. Those which back on to a church will often have a pleasant outlook and, of course, houses with a view from the upper windows can be nice where the conversion makes this the living area, with the bedrooms below.

A lot of old terraced houses are very narrow, with equally narrow staircases giving access to three or four levels. Prices are such that it is feasible to buy two, where they can be found side by side, and knock them into one. Similarly, those with larger budgets could buy a third, which could perhaps be demolished to make a garden or courtyard. This is not as unlikely as it sounds when the starting point might be a derelict ruin.

One near neighbour of ours has bought up a short street of about eight dwellings which will obviously end up as something quite special. Others have made an attractive and imaginative home from one small building which is ideal for holidays and inexpensive in terms of upkeep.

In a lot of old villages all over France, small farmers live in the village rather than outside it and keep all their tools, wagons, tractors and so on in the *remise* next door. This can usually be identified by its large double doors and narrow slits or a lack of windows altogether. The same applies to blacksmiths and other artisans. Where both home and *remise* come on the market the latter, being uninhabitable, but often the same size as the house, is usually very cheap. Although local planning restrictions may forbid changing the façade, the combination can make a very attractive proposition; the ground floor of the remise perhaps remaining as a garage, a rare asset in any town or village centre, with a floor installed above for accommodation. (*Remises* frequently have no dividing floor between ground and roof.) Depending on the area and climate, light can either be let in through roof windows, translucent panels, or a section of the roof can be removed completely to form a terrace. In some cases, despite internal alterations, if the façade remains untouched the *remise* can still be rated as agricultural. The same applies to some of the old roof-top *ateliers* – old town centre workshops with glass roofs which were once used for dressmaking, printing and other trades. An apartment conversion will let in plenty of light and frequently leaks as well, but with modern materials the former can be controlled and the latter cured.

Whilst on the subject of apartments, it is always desirable to buy the whole building if possible. A lot of old property is divided into apartments, but there is no such thing as a leasehold in France. Each is sold freehold and there is frequently no management or syndicate to sort out communal problems. Of course, these can usually be overcome eventually, but there is more peace of mind in owning a building all the way down to the ground it is standing on.

I speak from personal experience here, having bought a rather barn-like apartment on the top floor of a very old building dating back to the seventeenth century in Agde, a small town on the Gulf of Lyons historically rated as France's second oldest. (Only Marseilles is older, but both date back to Phoenician times.) It was literally four walls and a roof with no water or electricity supply and no sewage outlet, but it was cheap. Fortunately possessing the knowledge and tools to do the work myself I wasn't too daunted, even by the fact that the internal walls and ceilings had been knocked down with the resulting debris covering the floor to a depth of up to two feet. About thirty vanloads to the local tip (*décharge public*) cleared this initial rubble and revealed some rather nice tiles. Being a corner site there were windows on two sides and, in the course of removing the old plaster and rendering to repoint the stonework and thus strengthen the walls, another window, long since blocked up, became apparent and was duly opened up to give a splendid view of the cathedral and mountains beyond. So much for the bonuses: when the time came to apply to the water authority to connect up to water and sewage they told me their rules had changed three months before and that they couldn't! It really looked like six months hard labour converting a ruin into a rather nice apartment complete with a gallery level at the high end (five metres) had been a catastrophic blunder. A dry home – no water in and no sewage out. Nightmarish visions of carrying water up two flights of stairs in jerrycans filled at the town tap and surreptitious night journeys to empty a portable bucket-type toilet into the public lavatory.

After a short but very worrying period, both problems

were solved: the water supply by twisting the arm of my downstairs neighbour, who sold us the flat, to plumb into his supply and install our own private meter to apportion the bill; and the sewage by carefully tapping around the two foot thick external walls until a hollow, vertical channel was located. This, when the wall was opened up, proved to be the sewer pipe to the flat below which I was able to 'T' into. Panic over, but beware – a wiser buyer would have asked the right questions first.

Incidentally, the change of policy by the water authority was explained as being due to rising costs of installation. If a building has been divided into apartments, they will only supply one mains water inlet and one sewage outlet. The rest is up to individual owners to get out of trouble as best they can, and sort out the problem from there on. The difficulty is that the other owners might have lived undisturbed for years and don't want or need anyone plumbing in to their systems. No doubt they could be compelled by law, but apart from being costly this course of action is hardly likely to endear you to the neighbours. Remember, where essential services are lacking in an apartment (electricity is not usually a problem) you should make sure that it is possible to have them installed. This may mean obtaining a neighbour's permission to share, and it may also mean money changing hands, before you can sign on the dotted line.

Another aspect fraught with potential problems, especially for the owner of the top apartment, is the question of the roof. In a lot of cases repairs are paid for by that individual simply because of the impossibility of convincing anyone below that roof repairs concern them too. A good insurance should simplify this problem, but you might find that any repairs are covered under a guarantee which was provided by a local builder who did work on the roof in the past. The previous owner will often have had the roof made good, knowing that his investment would have soon deteriorated otherwise. In these cases the guarantee is sometimes valid for anything up to ten years, but was given verbally! Experience has shown that a lot of builders are quite meticulous in honouring their obligations, but something in writing as part of the purchase agreement makes for more peace of mind.

When contemplating property in the country, such as a

barn or farmhouse, the sewage system will often be in the form of a septic tank and the water supply will be provided by a well and pump, both of which will need vetting by an expert to make sure all is working properly. A septic tank (*fosse septique*) will sometimes need replacing which is not difficult. In these days of pollution, however, well water can become contaminated and needs careful testing. A local laboratory (common in France) can give an analysis.

Mains water supplies are becoming more available to outlying areas, at a price, so it pays to research the feasibility and the price of this before buying. Many towns and villages are expanding rapidly, especially those within striking distance of a major town or where holiday developments are taking place. This means they will have to be supplied with water and the routing of the supply may, with luck, pass close to your property. If this happens waste no time in contacting your regional water authority (*service d'eau*). It will be cheaper for you to be connected while the trenches are still open and the pipes are being laid. (Cheaper still if you dig the trench from them to you.) Once it has all been filled in the connection price will rise considerably. The same applies to the electricity. Where long distances are involved, connection can be costly.

Where to Buy
Choice of location may be governed by such factors as the need to be within easy travelling distances of elderly family or relatives, or local to business interests, but where there are no such limitations the choice is as diverse as the climatic extremes.

Some of the decision will depend on budget. For example, buying property near the sea, regardless of region, will always be more expensive than just a few miles inland. Close to a large town, especially Paris or any other major commercial centre, will cost more than in or around an outlying village or small town. Winter sports or summer holiday venues never come cheap, though some are dearer than others. For instance, the Gulf of Lyons – that area of the Mediterranean nearer the Spanish border, which has dozens of ports and marinas and is rapidly being developed – is much cheaper than the more fashionable Côte d'Azure.

Fashion is not the only factor involved here, though this is the largest wine producing area in Europe. Beziers, a thriving commercial town on the main motorway and rail routes between Paris and Spain and also on the Canal du Midi, is the wine capital of France. A title admittedly gained from the quantity of wine produced rather than the quality; this is where the EEC wine lakes are fermented and due to this vast overproduction the government has offered various encouragements to producers to change the crop to sunflowers (or similar) or sell off the land for other uses. The last few years have seen many former vineyards become housing estates. This has had the effect of leaving a lot of town and village centre property vacant and ripe for redevelopment – mostly at very low prices. By the same token a lot of the farm and outlying property, now no longer in use, is coming on to the market at bargain prices.

The Dordogne is another example of a formerly intensive agricultural region where many farms, together with outbuildings have been and are still being sold off. Always very popular with the British and also with the Germans. It is said that the Germans buy the farmhouses and the British buy the barns. Be that as it may, some of the latter make magnificent homes for their contented owners.

No doubt your eventual choice of location will be arrived at by travelling the country as much as possible, or it may be a place where you have enjoyed a holiday and are familiar with the region. One vital point to bear in mind, especially if your plan is to take up permanent residence is that a good holiday venue does not necessarily mean it is good for living there all year round. A small, perhaps delightful and picturesque village may have a completely different character when out of season. Many such places simply die for up to nine months of the year – this includes shops which often close down with everything else at the end of September. Property in this sort of area should always be viewed out of season, preferably during bad weather. If it suits you under those circumstances then the rest of the year has to be better.

Another point to bear in mind, especially if retirement is the plan, is the availability of economical shopping. In many rural areas, just like the UK, the local village shop, due to its lack of purchasing power, is usually expensive. While you are able to drive, of course, this doesn't present too much of a problem, as a choice of large national hypermarkets are often to be found within ten or twenty miles, on the outskirts of your local town. The problems start when you stop driving or when harsh winter weather keeps you isolated.

A retired friend of mine lived in a beautiful little village a few miles from Avignon. For a while all was well until she found that the village was dying around her. The young were moving to where they had better work opportunities and the elderly were, inevitably, getting older and dying. At the same time shops and other local facilities were closing down through lack of trade. At the age of seventy-two, having thought she had found the home in which she would stay for the rest of her life, she had to go through the whole process again and move to a small town where things were happening.

Whilst most towns are fairly cosmopolitan, some small villages are almost like large families, where all the inhabitants know each other and may resent 'foreigners' moving in. In small villages anywhere there is a certain reserve towards strangers, but in rare cases the atmosphere is much cooler. I know two local villages where the reception of outsiders is so extremely different, despite only being some ten kilometres apart. In one of them you could be forgiven for presuming a border has been crossed by mistake into a foreign and hostile land, whereas in the other, nothing is too much trouble when help or information is sought.

All these factors need to be determined before any commitment is made.

How to Buy (Part One)

This section can be broken into two parts: how to find a property and then how to go about buying it.

The most obvious way to achieve both aims is to walk into an estate agency (*agence immobilier*) in the region of your choice and ask to view the available property. A good and reputable agent will know the area well and should be able to advise on local facilities and give you some idea of what is permissible in the way of alterations and improvements.

Due to the growing trend of non-French buying property, it is getting easier to find an agency where English is spoken.

Many are large companies which have branches throughout France and with the use of Minitel (the French telephone computer link) they can give you information say on what is available in the Dordogne while you are in their office in Paris, or vice versa.

I have nothing against estate agents, most of whom, but not all, do their job conscientiously and well. They also take anything up to ten per cent of the purchase price (reducing to five per cent on very expensive properties), mostly from the vendor, but in some regions it is split between buyer and vendor. This would seem a lot, but it is not all profit, a good proportion of it goes in taxes. Nevertheless, it amounts to a considerable sum and as a lot of vendors would prefer to keep this for themselves, they opt for a private sale, methods of which will be discussed later.

When dealing with estate agents, bear in mind that those operating a good and successful business will not be relying on your purchase to save them from financial collapse. They should therefore not need to push or pressurize you into buying. Like anyone else, they want to do business, but beware those who seem to exist to convince enthusiastic foreign buyers that the price they are being asked is really the bargain of the month and that a whole queue of other eager clients are merely waiting for the first sign of hesitation to pounce and snatch the sale away from under your nose.

One of the first things to find out is how long the property has been on the market, especially when subjected to this kind of pressure. Even if your heart is set on a particular place a measure of caution is advisable. It may be true that you have found a real bargain at a very low price, but this is highly unlikely to happen through an agent, who will already have advised the vendor on the likely selling price.

A good agent will show you around the property and let you make up your own mind. Some even give you a cooling off period in case you change it later or find somewhere even better. One thing to bear in mind is that gazumping is illegal in France. If a house is under offer to a client, no further offers will be accepted unless the first falls through.

It is only by visiting as many properties as possible that one begins to get the 'feel' of prices and values and this experience is vital for purchasing at a realistic price. Most good agents have many properties on their lists and should not therefore try to influence you to buy any particular one. If they do, beware.

Due to the rising popularity of buying homes in France, a lot of enterprising UK estate agents are starting to include French property on their lists. Enquiries near home, therefore, could decide the area you choose for your next holiday.

Another way to buy is to buy privately. An exploration of the streets and alleys of any old town or village will show the odd house for sale. The usual sign just says *A Vendre* with a telephone number. It is quite likely that the owner will speak French only and if it happens that you don't and the place you have found looks interesting, a translator might be needed. Even if this service must be paid for, you will probably find that it is still worthwhile as the asking price is bound to be less than through an agent. Those with some French should at least be able to find out the price and thus establish whether it is worth proceeding with.

When talking price with a French person, especially the older generation, bear in mind that many still talk in terms of the old currency. This will add a startling amount of zeros to the price and may easily frighten away the uninitiated. If in doubt, ask for the price to be written down, preferably in New Francs. If this request proves incomprehensible to the vendor, and it sometimes does, a translator will be needed to clarify the situation.

Although this method entails a lot of legwork, it has the advantage of acquainting you with the neighbourhood before needing to make any decisions. When you feel the need to rest, there is usually a handy bar whose owner probably knows everything that is going on locally including which houses are for sale and if he doesn't one of his regulars probably will. I have always been amazed by the numbers of Britons living all over France and an enquiry in the village bar will often lead to directions and even an introduction. A lot of useful local knowledge can be gained in this way.

Most large supermarkets have a free advertising area for customers which is usually in the form of a board covered in postcard size adverts. This is often useful not only for finding property for private sale but also for second hand furniture and appliances etc. Lastly, a lot of small shops will have a pile of free advertising newspapers by the till. These are usually regional and a very good source of finding likely places to view.

One particular problem which frequently arises in a private sale is where the owner wants to avoid paying taxes. Maybe he has inherited the property and it now being his second home he will have to pay Capital Gains Tax when he sells it. Now if there is one thing the French really hate doing it is paying tax in any form and avoidance is a sort of national sport.

The first thing you will notice in one of those deals is that the owner will suggest two prices, the lower of which will be the 'official' price and the higher one the actual price, with the difference to be made up in cash. He will probably point out that in this way you will also be making savings as the *notaire* will only be informed of the official price and thus the ten per cent you have to pay him will subsequently be reduced. This is true, in fact, so it will be left up to your own judgement as to whether the risk is worth it. Many vendors wouldn't dream of selling the property any other way, so if you have set your heart on the property in question the temptation might be strong. There are, however, a few other factors you should bear in mind. First of all, if this is to be your second property (even if your principal residence is in the UK) and you decide to sell within twenty-two years (although there is a substantial reduction after five) you will be liable for Capital Gains Tax. (This won't come in bill form, but will be deducted by the *notaire* in his capacity as tax collector for the government.) If, therefore, the purchase price was artificially low, the apparent gain will be more than the actual gain and so you will lose out in the end.

Secondly, in some areas, especially in the case of old property in conservation zones, the *mairie* (town hall) is automatically offered first refusal on any home coming on to the market. Thus if the official price is made too attractive there is always the risk that they will take up their option at that price plus ten per cent, so the vendor has no choice but to sell. After all, he can hardly claim to have made a mistake and forgotten a zero! Of course, it is the vendor who suffers mostly in a case such as this, but you as the buyer will have to start searching all over again, and if by any chance you have been persuaded to part with a cash deposit, you are going to find it very difficult if not impossible to recover. Although the law will tend to come down more heavily on the vendor, your case is unlikely to arouse much sympathy.

Thirdly, another aspect of this, to call a spade a spade, sharp practice in the case of really cheap property – a ruin for instance – is that the Notaire will often have a minimum charge. Thus if you have been asked to pay, say, 60,000 francs on the basis of 40,000 francs officially and 20,000 francs cash and the *notaire*'s basic minimum is 6,000f., then this is what you will have to pay regardless, even if it works out at twenty per cent, so the risk you have taken will have been entirely for the benefit of the vendor. Alas, not many properties are still available for these sort of prices, but there are a few, especially uninhabitable ruins, some of which have fine potential.

Whilst on the subject of price, it would be as well to point out at this stage that whether or not the purchase of an old or run down dwelling is actually an economical project depends on how much of the work you intend to carry out personally. If all the work is to be contracted out to a builder you might find that it would have been cheaper to have bought a new place at the start. New homes are also very good value in France. This book concerns the restoration of old property however large or small and is aimed towards those who like living in traditional and characteristic surroundings which are impossible to find in anything new. In this case the expense is justified, but it would be a mistake to buy somewhere old just because the initial price was attractive.

Perhaps the one exception would be where money had to be borrowed to buy a new home, but a ruin could be afforded for cash, although this would not always apply. Should the building be in a state that could pose danger to passers by, or to buildings around it, there might be a time limit set by the authorities for the essential work to be carried out. Otherwise there is nothing to stop you from leaving the repairs until such time as the funds are available to do the work, during which time you will have a slowly appreciating asset. It all depends on how much of a hurry you are in to complete and inhabit your acquisition.

The subject of retiring to or taking up permanent residence in France is too complex to be covered here. For help in this respect you could do no better than buy a copy of *Living in France* by Philip Holland whose comprehensive and interesting book is a must to anyone contemplating the move.

How to Buy (Part Two)

Having decided on a particular property and agreed a price with the vendor, the next step is normally a meeting at the *notaire* to enter into a contract, both parties being present.

If you are absolutely certain you wish to go ahead, you will be asked to sign a *compromis de vente*, which will also be signed by the vendor. This is your agreement to buy and the vendor's agreement to sell. At the same time you will be asked to pay a ten per cent deposit and it is very important that this should be subject to obtaining satisfactory searches, necessary finance and finding no major structural problems when the building is inspected (if an inspection is intended).

The *compromis de vente*, once signed in the presence of the *notaire*, is legally binding to both parties, and so gives you full protection against gazumping.

Should you feel fairly sure, but want time for reflection, it is possible to get the vendor to sign a *promesse de vente* against a deposit of ten per cent. Your time for thought will have to be agreed on though, and if, for any reason you decide to opt out, there is no guarantee of recovering your deposit.

At the meeting you should get a rough idea of when completion should be and will probably be questioned as to how you intend to pay the balance and whether you intend to get a mortgage and so on. Completion normally takes around three months and during this time the payment of the balance can be transferred from your UK bank into the *notaire's* business account. You will be expected to be present for signing at completion, but to avoid the expense of possibly wasted journeys you can, at the first meeting, invest the *notaire* with power of attorney to sign on your behalf.

A word about the *notaire*. Part lawyer, part government official, he or she is the only lawyer in France empowered to register the transfer of property. As such, unlike the system in the UK, where both parties use a different solicitor for conveyancing, the same *notiare* can act impartially for both vendor and buyer.

The chances are that you will not know of a *notaire* and one will be suggested to you by the vendor. This is normal practice and should not present any problems. If, however, you have any reason or desire to use a different one, you are quite at liberty to do so. (A list of *notaires* can be found at the *mairie* or the *syndicate d'initiative* (information office).) After all, you as the buyer are going to be footing the bill, which will be at least ten per cent (varying with local taxes) of the purchase price. Should your decision mean that two *notaires* are involved, the fees should remain the same and the *notaires* have to share.

There is no problem these days in transferring funds from the UK, but, of course, you might already have an account in France, in which case you will not be likely to lose out if the exchange rate suddenly goes against you. With sufficient time and planning the transfer can be made to your French account when the rate is favourable.

It is also possible nowadays to get a mortgage from a French bank. For example, the *Credit Lyonnais* has a London office where it can all be arranged in English currency. At the time of writing they are willing to finance up to eighty per cent of the cost for a fee of one per cent, about 3,000 francs (£300). This is normally for a period of twenty years. It is difficult to quote interest rates as they obviously fluctuate, but they would appear to be quite competitive.

For those with a longer term plan, there is another much cheaper way to borrow money from a French bank which works more like a building society in that you start a savings account (*epargne logement*) by paying in an initial lump sum – maybe 1,500 francs (approximately £150) and then regular monthly payments of 300 francs (approximately £30). After a specified period, usually not less than eighteen months, the bank will make you a fixed period loan of around 100,000 francs (approximately £10,000) for as little as five per cent. In the case of a joint husband and wife savings account the loan can be doubled.

Of course, all these figures are subject to variation, but if you are in no great hurry to buy, the scheme is well worth investigating by comparing the rates offered by the major banks. Although eighteen months sounds like a long time, for those whose search time is limited to occasional holidays that length of time may be taken up finding the right place. Alternatively you may have the necessary funds to buy and then the loan would come in very useful for making the necessary improvements when the waiting period has elapsed.

Most mortgage companies will require a structural survey and/or a valuation before loaning money. They may indeed arrange this as part of the agreement. Obviously with the possibility of repossession in view, they will need to be satisfied that the value is realistic. Even if you are not borrowing money, you will be well advised, unless you have the necessary expertise, to have a survey done. The problem is, that there is no such thing as a surveyor in France. Thus the best course of action is to consult a local architect, who is likely to be well versed in old property in the locality and its inherent problems.

A simple valuation can normally be arranged by the *notaire*, but only on demand. It is as well to know that the *notaire* is in no way responsible for the value or structure of the building, it is for the buyer to beware.

It will be noticed that when the deal has gone through, the title to the property, if you are married, will be under the husband's surname and the wife's maiden name.

Finally a word of warning, which is not as ridiculous as it may sound, and applies especially in the south: don't be in a hurry to make a decision after a long, fatiguing drive, or make any decisions at all after a lunch including the very pleasant but equally soporific local wine, especially in very hot weather. Under these circumstances it is possible to enter into a deal in a state of complete bemusement not at all recommended for making major investments.

As it is likely you will live many travelling hours from your new acquisition, it makes a lot of sense to view it as many times as possible. It is very easy, once back in the UK, to forget much of the detail. Also, if agent or owner is present at the viewing they are very apt to spend so much time trying to sell the place that you will be concentrating more on trying to understand them rather than actually looking. If at all possible, ask to be left alone to view at your leisure and take photos, sketches and measurements as an aid to remembering all the essential details later on.

Further advice on all aspects of buying property in France can be obtained from a property consultant, several of whom advertise in the property section of the national Sunday newspapers and other publications.

Some consultants specialize in a particular region and others have offices all over France. They exist specifically to help the British buyer over the various hurdles encountered when buying, financing and insuring properties. Above all, they help with language difficulties. Naturally they charge for the service, but those lacking the confidence to go it alone, so to speak, could do a lot worse than to enlist the services of someone who will be very experienced and able to handle whichever part of a purchase you would like them to assist with. They can even deal with the entire operation including builder's estimates, keeping an eye on the progress and, afterwards the maintenance of house, garden, swimming pool and so on.

2   The Town Hall

Part of the agreement to buy a property may be subject to successfully obtaining planning permission for various alterations or building projects. Even if this is not the case it is very likely that you will wish to make some changes. France is not unlike the UK in this respect, in that any major and some minor work – especially to the exterior – will require a permit. This gives the authorities a measure of control over the safety aspects of rebuilding and in areas of historic or architectural interest they are able to preserve the character.

Generally speaking, any reasonable request will receive a sympathetic hearing, but where buildings are classified as being of historical importance, as is sometimes the case in very old towns, any proposed changes to the façade will come under very close scrutiny. Often in these areas the regulations are so strict that there is even a limitation on the number of colours acceptable for the windows and shutters.

Having said that though, it is quite evident when looking around some old towns and villages that many owners have gone ahead without official consultation, have made quite radical changes and have apparently got away with it. One could, therefore, be forgiven for trying the same thing. After all, dealing with local councils can be a bit trying even without the additional strain posed by language problems. All that can be said is that the authorities in some areas are stricter than others. Also, a change of *maire* (mayor) can completely alter previously lax attitudes, especially in ancient towns where the whole charm and character is in danger of being eroded or lost for ever. In these days of rapid change, the preservation of old buildings is attracting a lot more interest than it did twenty or even ten years ago. For your own peace of mind and economy it is better to ask first.

Failure to do so could result in your being required to put things back how they were at your, often very considerable, expense and within a given time limit. The authorities have been known to get extremely unpleasant with those who just go ahead and do their own thing.

The first move is to visit the *mairie*, or *hôtel de ville* as the town hall is sometimes known. It is usually well signposted and easily identified by the one or more French tricolour (red, white and blue) flags flying above the entrance. Once inside there will be an *accueil* or reception point indicated. If the property in question is within the boundaries of the town, your enquiry will be dealt with by the *service d'urbanisme*. This department will normally be run by a qualified architect who is thoroughly familiar with all the old buildings under his control.

Should the enquiry relate to property in a small village or out in the country, it will be dealt with by the nearest office of the *Ministère de l'Équipment du Logement des Transports et de la Mer*. In some cases this may be in or near the *mairie*, or you may have to go to the main town of the county (*département*). Either way the *mairie* will be able to direct you to the right person.

It is not possible to list here all the alterations or building projects which might be permissable, so the following should be taken as a rough guide only. Policies, by-laws and regulations change from time to time and from region to region. Each area is zoned: urban, suburban, rural and so on. It is quite possible that an invisible boundary passes between your home and a neighbour's, making regulations applicable to one property different to the other, even with regard to such mundane things as siting a car port or garden shed. This is why it is vital to find out the law relating to your own property and/or land rather than accept possible misinformation from someone who is unqualified.

Generally speaking permission will be necessary for the following:

1. Any sort of extension, including vertical (i.e. adding height to a building to make more accommodation).
2. Construction of a mezzanine floor or converting a loft (*grenier*) into living space. (All living space is chargeable

by the square metre where the headroom is more than 1.8m, so any changes which add to the square meterage mentioned on the deeds raise the *tax foncière*.)

3. Conversion of any non dwelling into a dwelling (i.e. barns (*granges*) and other agricultural buildings such as workshops (*ateliers*) garages (*remises*) wine cellars, etc.).

4. Adding a garage, including temporary car port or shed.

5. Construction of a balcony. In some conservation areas this will be forbidden or strictly controlled in terms of size and design of the railings (*garde-corpes*).

6. Opening up windows where none existed or enlarging existing windows. (This will frequently depend on local by-laws, some of which state that any new window within 3m of a neighbour's house would require written consent from the owner to go with the planning application.

7. Changing the window style (i.e. multi plane to single pane to admit more light. This may not be allowed in conservation zones where everything must be kept compatible with the period architecture as far as possible.)

8. Changing the type of roof tiles. (France is very proud of her regional roof styles, so with traditional buildings one is usually encouraged to keep to the original type, all of which are available in synthetic materials as well as the real thing. The latter can also be found second-hand which looks more authentic.)

9. Changing the external colour of walls, windows and shutters (in some historic zones).

10. Removing rendering to expose stonework, either in part or completely. (In some cases, the general stonework is not particularly attractive and just the large corner blocks and aperture lintels are left exposed, and the rest rendered.)

11. Covering existing exposed stonework with rendering. (This might not be allowed where all the other houses have exposed stonework.)

12. Installing a roof terrace. (This practice is mostly applicable to town or village centre dwellings without gardens or the possibility of balconies. Part of the roof is removed, the walls and floor below waterproofed and

drained. [see chapter 8] This is usually allowed even in historic zones as the façade is left intact and the terrace is not visible from the road. The removal is often limited to thirty per cent of the roof area. Permission would normally only be refused if the terrace was overlooked by a neighbour who objected.)

13. Replacing very old front doors. (Obviously this may be essential where the original door is no longer serviceable, but in some zones the new door would have to conform to the traditional style.)

14. Opening up a normal size access door in a large garage door where the garage has been converted into a dwelling. (This would normally be allowed, but if the doors open on to the street this might affect the rateable value of the conversion.)

15. Installing iron security grills. (In some zones these must conform to the traditional style.)

16. Installing solar panels or large dish TV aerials. (Permission normally required in conservation zones only.)

17. Erecting walls or fences where none existed, or where an old stone wall is in ruins, replacing it with a new wall or fence. (If the ruined stone wall is a local feature, a grant might be forthcoming to help restore it.)

18. Removal of established trees too close to house and blocking light.

19. Drilling a well, installing a septic tank or swimming pool. (The well water must be analysed at required intervals. Laboratories are to be found in most towns.) Directions from any pharmacy, the tourist information centre, or *mairie*.

20. Siting a mobile home in the garden.

21. Storing chemicals and foul smelling, toxic/inflammable substances on the premises. (Permission would depend on location and proximity of other dwellings.)

22. Starting up a kennels or keeping pigs. (This would not be allowed next to an existing house.)

The list goes on. Hopefully, this cross-section will demonstrate the sort of things planning permission will be required for.

Internal changes are of less importance to the *mairie*, but major work, involving the removal of walls or other structural supports will still need a permit as a means of controlling the integrity of the building. Unless you are qualified to know which walls are load bearing, your plans will need to be backed by drawings from an architect. This is especially important in the case of an apartment, where an unqualified person could endanger the building or indeed those which are adjoining. If proved negligent, any damage caused to other property will be your responsibility and for this reason, when insuring the dwelling, make sure you are covered for accidental damage to others. Although a lot of all-risk house policies include such clauses, not all do, and in any event if the damage was caused by negligence the insurance company may not be willing to pay out. The best advice is: if in any doubt whatsoever, ask.

One thing to bear in mind when getting planning permission is that the permit, when issued, has a fixed life, usually one year. Although it is most unlikely to be refused if a new application is made for the same project, it has been known to happen due to some change in regulations. An example of this could be when a permit has been issued for an extension adding 100m^2 to the floor area. If after a year, only 50m^2 have been added and a new law has been passed limiting extensions in the zone to 50m^2, the work will be halted. As I said, this would be a rare occurrence, but illustrates the point that if whatever project you wish a permit for is pushing the limit of what is allowable, it might be a good idea to get it done quickly.

Grants

As in the UK, grants are sometimes available for various aspects of home improvement. This is very much a local government matter and so it is impossible to predict the situation in your particular district. The *mairie* will be able to tell you what, if anything, they are prepared to pay. Also, any change of local or national government can alter the position – for better or worse.

In Agde, being very old and therefore of historical interest, a grant of twenty-five per cent may be claimed (1991) for approved work on the façade. Naturally there are conditions attached. To qualify, the work has to be carried out by a registered builder. The money, paid out after the work has been completed (you have to pay the bill first and wait for the grant) must be paid into a French bank account. It is easy enough to start up a French bank account, mostly by walking in and asking, but this policy excludes the DIY enthusiast from claiming. The reason given for this is that it might encourage 'black' labour, from which the government would receive no taxes. Thus they pay it out with one hand and recover it with the other. *C'est la vie*! At least if you are getting all the work done by a registered builder you can claim some back for the façade.

In different regions grants may be available for such things as installation of bathrooms etc. It is always worth asking.

Incidentally, a lot of builders claim to be registered and can even show printed cards and letter headings. A genuine artisan of any trade will have a TVA (VAT) number. Beware of those who don't, and require the whole payment in cash. Although it may be done out of ignorance, it is illegal to employ 'black' labour. The labourer is frowned on by the authorities, who are unable to do much about it due to the numbers involved, but the employer is meant to know about these things and can be liable to prosecution.

It pays, therefore, to employ bona fide tradesmen and to be meticulous about keeping all bills from them, and any you get for the purchase of materials. All these things are deductable against Capital Gains Tax should you sell the property. Those doing the work themselves can now benefit from a recent law. The deduction for your labour is the cost of materials multiplied by three. It is thus unnecessary to log your hours apart from personal interest and to give an idea of how long the next project will take.

Whether you have left the job in the hands of a local architect or are paying the builders and tradesmen yourself, it is quite normal for an advance to be demanded for the purchase of materials, and at various stages thereafter until completion. It is also not a bad idea to pay the final instalment only after you are satisfied that everything is properly finished to your satisfaction.

Local Architects

If you decide to leave the work to be supervised by an architect, which could end up saving you money on repeated journeys from the UK to check up on progress, always use a locally based one. Not only will they be very familiar with the property, but if they are involved with travelling any distance to supervise it will inevitably cost more. They will know the local builders well and be able to give you an accurate estimate (*devis*) which will remain current for six months. On major work which is likely to take longer the estimate may be good for a year, as costs are fairly steady at the moment.

Some architects will supply drawings for DIY builders, but they don't usually give advice, because it is very difficult to cost such a thing. If they are employed to see the whole project through to the end, they will be able to deal with planning permission, and thus save you having to brave the *mairie*. They will also know when not to waste your money by asking permission for things that will not be allowed.

Free Advice

For those who have bought an old property and wish to restore it back to original, there are various forms of help available. The *Agence National pour Amelioration d'Habitat* (ANAH), for instance, exists to encourage owners (of any nationality) of old property to renovate it rather than let it deteriorate beyond repair. This agency can be contacted through the *mairie* or *prefecture*, as can the *Architect Conseil de Bâtiment de France*.

Some old towns of noted historic interest have their own preservation societies. These are often voluntary organisations working in conjunction with the *mairie*, who will be only too pleased to give interested owners advice on local buildings and approved aspects of restoration. Agde, for example has a society known as ARVA (*Association pour le Rehabilitation de Vieille Agde*).

Enquiries to find out about these and other useful organisations should be made at the *mairie*, the local tourist information office, or *Syndicate d'Initiative* as it is sometimes called, or at the local library, which will also contain a selection of useful books on traditional buildings, for reference.

The following is the form which is obtainable from the *mairie* for building work not needing a full construction permit.

Ministere de l'Equipment, du Logement Des Transports et de la Mer.

DÉCLARATION DE TRAVAUX EXEMPTES DE PERMIS DE CONSTRUIRE OU DÉCLARATION DE CLÔTURE. (Article L. 422-2 ou L 441-2 du Code de l'Urbanisme)

COMMENT REMPLIR CE FORMULAIRE? (How to fill in the form. You are advised to press hard with a black ball-point pen on a hard surface so that all the self-carboned copies are filled in at once. You may detach and keep the bottom copy.)

RENSEIGNEMENTS PARTICULIERS A CERTAINES RUBRIQUES (information concerning certain headings)

Heading 1. '*Le déclarant*' is the owner or the person entitled to do the work.

Heading 2. '*Le terrain*' is the owned land formed by one parcel or adjacent parcels belonging to the same owner, or joint owners.

Heading 32:

32.1 This concerns modifications to roofs (e.g. roof terrace) shop fronts and opening up or enlarging windows.

32.2 This concerns, for example, installing of posts or pylons more than 12m high, walls more than 2m high, also swimming pools.

32.3 This concerns the addition of a balcony, creation of an additional dwelling room, (i.e. conversion of *grenier*) siting of a garden shed or garage or workshop or an exterior lift cage etc., none being more than 20m^2 in surface area.

32.5 This form does not replace the permit required (according to article 9 of the law of 31 December 1913 relating to historic monuments) which should be applied for from the regional director of cultural affairs. (The *mairie* will explain where.)

32.6 This concerns light leisure dwellings without foundations, collapsible and transportable (i.e. mobile homes etc.) for temporary siting on a registered camp-site which are more than 35m^2 in surface area.

Heading 33 This is a calculation of the total living space of the dwelling, including balconies, roof terraces etc., to work out any tax changes in respect of modifications (*taxes foncieres* etc.)

DANS TOUT LES CAS: IN ALL CASES: (the following is required)
A plan of the situation of the terrain, including the roads. Scale between 1/5000 and 1/25000. (This can be obtained from the land registry (*cadastre*) Your *notaire* could advise.)
A three-dimensional plan of the proposed construction on a scale between 1/50 and 1/500, showing in particular the distances of the construction from the boundaries and other buildings on the site. A plan of the façades to be modified; scale 1/50 or 1/100, or photographs showing the existing state and modifications planned.
If it concerns a wall or other form of enclosure, a plan including measurements and the proposed building material.

DANS CERTAIN CAS: IN CERTAIN CASES:
1. If the '*declarent*' is not the owner of the land or building he must be able to show the authorization from the owner to carry out the work.
2. If the '*declarent*' whether or not the owner of the land asks a third party to complete the declaration by proxy, the third party will need signed authorization.
3. If the work necessitates the felling and clearing of trees in the forests or parks subject to the article L 130-1 of the *code de l'urbanisme* of articles L 311-1 or 312-1 of the *code forestier*, authorization will be required.
4. If the work necessitates an authorization of occupation of public land this authorization must be included with the application.

COMMENT ET OU DEPOSER LA DECLARATION ET LE DOSSIER?
HOW AND WHERE TO TAKE THIS DECLARATION AND PLANS ETC.

All documents plus three copies of the plans should be taken to the *mairie* by hand, or sent by registered post (*lettre recommande*) with a request for an acknowledgement of receipt.

Within one month from the date the authorities (*mairie* or *préfeture*) received the plans they should let you know if they are opposed to them or if they intend to impose certain limitations. In some cases, where the involvement of other authorities is necessary, because of laws relating to access, historic monuments etc., this might be increased to two months. In this case you will be informed within the month. Should you hear nothing by the time the month is up you are free to begin the work.

3 Transport

Very few properties have the benefit of a tip within wheelbarrow distance or a building supply merchant next door, so when estimating budgets, those intending to do some or all of the work themselves will find that transport is essential.

It is always staggering to see the vast amount of dust and rubble produced by a fairly minor demolition job, so unless space is unlimited a regular clearance is necessary. Fortunately every town (even small ones) has a local tip where up to a ton at a time can usually be dumped without charge.

Of course, clearance can be arranged in other ways; skips are available in some areas, though not so widely used as in the UK. This service will also depend on access. A lot of old town and village centre houses are in streets which are far too narrow for a skip. Also, it is likely that regular amounts of rubble wll need clearing over quite a long period, making the process quite costly. Some owners enlist the services of local farmers or wine growers whose tractors and trailers are lying idle (especially when the harvest or *vendange* is over). The problem here is that the clearance might be needed at the wrong time.

Collection of materials is another problem as it often needs to be done quickly to save holding a job up. So one way and another it is better to be independent.

The nature of the transport used will depend on several factors: How long is the project likely to take? How near is the local tip and builders' merchant? Has the property got access for a vehicle? (A lot of town and village centre property is in very narrow alleys or areas where cars are prohibited.) How much are you prepared to spend? And so on.

36

Starting off with economy in mind, or where access is limited, there is an excellent type of hand cart available in France. It can be pushed or pulled, by hand, bicycle or moped and has wheels large enough to cope with bad surfaces. A sound model can cope with a bag of cement or 50kg of sand. They usually measure 60cm by 40cm. They were in widespread use until fairly recently by smallholders, allotment owners and small wine growers until EEC allowances enabled many of these people to acquire more sophisticated transport. They are still, however, being used by the older generation in many places.

Going up market a little, a small quarter ton trailer (box type) is a very practical solution as it can be towed by a small family car and left 'on site' in your absence. An added benefit is that the inevitable dents and scratches arising from carrying rubble or building materials affect the trailer only. They are not, however, very good at carrying long lengths of timber. To some extent this problem can be overcome with a strong roof rack, but this can cause strain and damage to the roof. A good, waterproof cover is very useful protection for paper cement bags.

A strong estate car can carry most things and is likely to have good roof rack possibilities. It is also a reasonable vehicle in which to drive to France and back if your working time is limited to holidays. Unless well protected though, the re-sale value is going to drop considerably by the time the work is finished. One practical solution is to make a plywood box large enough to cover the floor area, with a front and two sides slightly higher than the front seat backs. Leave the back open for easy loading and carry a length of timber around 6cm x 7cm section which can lie across the back end of the box to support long lengths of timber. These can be stacked on the passenger side from the screen out through the open back door without inconvenience or damage to the seats. Avoid heavy braking though, and with a metre or two sticking out, care is needed reversing.

The ultimate transport is a van, which will be tough and able to carry more weight than a car. It will not be so pleasant for long journeys though. To maintain the condition, it still pays dividends to make a plywood box to protect the metalwork, stop rubbish from falling down behind the front seats and retain the wood carrying capability.

Whichever form of transport is chosen though, try to avoid the very real temptation to overload it with building materials. The tendency to do this can become almost compulsive on Saturday evenings near to closing time when you are stocking up with materials for working with on Sunday. A Monday 'fête day' makes the desire even stronger. Cement, plaster and ceramic tiles are all well known suspension breakers. Two or more journeys are more productive than one breakdown. Also, the French police are apt to frown on dangerously overloaded vans staggering along the road.

A van, like a box trailer, is something you may wish to leave in France if your property has a secure garage. Bear in mind though that a vehicle registered in the UK can officially remain in France for six months only before it must be imported. Enquire at the *mairie* for details.

If the purchase price was cheap enough it might pay to give the government the 18.6% (importation charge) to save bringing it to and fro, but bear in mind that there will then be a charge for the administrative work involved in changing the number plates, as well as the cost of the plates themselves. It will also mean that the car has to be insured in France, which is more expensive than the UK and when its usefulness has expired it will be more difficult to sell locally, being right-hand drive.

A few of these problems are solved by buying the van in France, but in some areas you will need residential status before being allowed to own a French registered vehicle. In the Dordogne, for instance, it is sufficient to obtain a *certificate d'Habitation* free from the *mairie*.

There is now an MOT test in France known as the *Controle Technique* and is obligatory for all French registered cars over four years old. Although very comprehensive (even covering exhaust emission levels) old vehicles seem to be given a more lenient pass standard and only fail on faulty brakes, lights, steering and tyres. Once through the test, proof and date of passing are displayed on the windscreen and in the *carte grise* (log book). Failed vehicles have eight weeks to rectify any faults and be re-tested. There is at least one *Controle Technique* centre in every town.

Registration of French vehicles is done by the *département* (county) whose postal code (usually the first two numbers) will be the last two on the number plate. Buying a vehicle outside the *département* will mean having the number plates changed, with the inevitable administrative charges, so it is always best to buy within the county.

To transfer the *carte grise* into your name it will be necessary to visit the *mairie*, who will ask for the money (around £20) in cheque form. If you don't have a local bank account it will have to be paid by *mandat*, a sort of postal order available at the PTT (post office). The *mairie* won't accept cash. It is at this point you may be asked for proof of residency. The PTT will require the exact address and *département* to fill in the *mandat*, so if in doubt ask at the *mairie* first and avoid extra trips between the two. Of course, obtaining residency may be no more than a formality, especially if you are an EEC National. If, however, the acquisition of your property is just for holidays, and you have no intention of living in France permanently, then to state that you are 'visiting', with a UK registered vehicle, may be simpler.

Assuming that you are buying a French registered vehicle, it will be necessary to insure it locally, as few UK companies will give you an unlimited green card (an additional insurance imposed by UK companies to cover travel abroad). As the *carte grise* must be in your possession before insurance can be organized, one is often faced with the paradoxical situation where you will not be able to drive on the road legally from the point of purchase to the insurance company's nearest branch. Hopefully they will not be too far apart as you will usually find a selection of 'assurance' offices in each town.

The basic insurance ('assurance' in France) is *responsabilité civil* – the equivalent of third party. This can be added to with fire and theft cover and also personal accident etc, or you can be covered comprehensively (*tout risques*). There are also additional breakdown recovery options which usually start to operate once over 50km from home address. Although more expensive than the UK, the cover note is also a green card, so there is no need to ask for special cover when crossing borders within the EEC and some others which are specified.

Road tax is much cheaper on the other hand and is cut in half once the vehicle is over five years old. It is based on 'horsepower', which is a fiscal measurement these days, the lowest group (as for insurance) being up to 4hp. This includes the Renault 4L, Citroen 2CV and 3CV (Dyane, 2CV6 etc). The disc (*vignette*) which is stuck on to the windscreen as proof of each year's payment is available, oddly enough, at any *tabac*, (tobacco shop) usually from mid November until early December, on production of the *carte grise*. The last date will be mentioned in newspapers and on TV and anyone missing it will have to apply at the *mairie* and pay an additional sum as a punishment for being late.

A portion of the insurance form must also be displayed on the windscreen. The company will provide a small plastic holder which has adhesive on one side.

Finally, in old quarters where delivery to the front door is impossible, a good, strong porters' trolley is invaluable. For carrying cement it should be lined with a plywood base and back which will help to prevent the paper sacks splitting. Bulk sand is best carried in buckets which will stack. A visit to the tip, frequently a rewarding experience, will often result in the acquisition of plastic or tin containers of the type that 10l. or 20l. of paint come in. They are also useful for carrying rubble and dust as they help to contain it and keep the amount of mess to a minimum. Any that are cleanable and still have their lids make good, dry storage for plaster and cement which would otherwise be at risk of solidifying in damp weather.

4 Finding Tradesmen

Anyone who has had building work done usually has a story to tell – sometimes good, sometimes horrific. Whichever the case, their knowledge can be put to good use in establishing who to use and who to avoid.

There is nothing as good as a personal recommendation, so it will pay you to ask around and seek out someone who can advise. It will also be beneficial at this stage to have some knowledge of the French language, including building terms and materials (see glossary at end of the book) or at least to have a friend who does. Not many local builders can speak English.

As for who to select, this will depend on the size of job and the amount of time that you will be there to supervise. For extensive work where your frequent presence is impossible, it may be advisable to ask a local architect to carry out this job for you. His fee can be balanced against the travelling costs you would have otherwise incurred. Alternatively, there are building consultants who perform the same task and work under titles such as *surveillance de bâtiment* or *bâtiment conseil*. The *mairie* will be able to provide addresses, but will sometimes be unwilling to give recommendations as they are supposed to be impartial. If the property was bought through an agent, they will be able to advise you and if they are local to the area they will certainly have a good knowledge of builders and other tradesmen in the district. The *notaire* can also prove to be a useful source of information.

British (or English-speaking) property consultants advertise in the UK papers which list property for sale abroad. Many of these consultants are based in France and can be a great help to the non-French speaker. You may have already used a consultant to find the property. Another aspect of their operation is to find builders and other tradesmen and oversee the work.

Those who are going to be on the spot for all or most of the time, can speak some French and haven't been able to find any satisfactory recommendations will have to do it the hard way, which is sometimes also the most interesting. Tradesmen advertise their services in numerous ways. One place in which to look is the French Yellow Pages trade directory. Better still, if you have a Minitel, the electronic phone directory which is also a computer terminal, this will do most of the searching for you once you have mastered its complexities.

The local papers can help, especially the free papers which are found on the counters of *boulangeries* and other shops. Tradesmen's business cards are also often to be found among the *petites annonces* usually located near the check-outs of supermarkets and DIY stores, or in local shops stuck on the back (the customer's side) of the till.

They will often have a remise somewhere in the town or village where they store all their equipment. This will usually have a plaque which gives the name, trade and telephone number. (e.g. *artisan maçon* – builder, *artisan carreleur* – ceramic tiling specialist and so on) and a telephone number.

There may, of course, be a delay before any work can be started as a good tradesman is invariably busy. Bear in mind, especially in the south, that a promise to come tomorrow should not be taken literally. It really means as soon as possible. Accepting this will save a lot of frustration.

However large or small the job is, an estimate (preferably two or three) is essential before making any agreement. Be sure to make it absolutely clear that you want an estimate only, at this stage. It is not unheard of for a tradesman to assume the job is his and turn up with his tools early the next morning.

With some trades, such as rendering, plastering and ceramic tiling, the estimate will come in the form of a set price per square metre. A busy (which usually means good) tradesman will often quote higher when he doesn't need the work, so getting to know the 'going rate' by getting other estimates will help you to decide who to use.

With electricians and plumbers especially it is important to have some knowledge of the sizes of wires and pipe for each purpose to avoid future snags. (Specifications to be found in Chapters 13 and 15.) A good example is copper pipe, the price of which increases with it's size, so the smaller bore the pipe, the cheaper it is. Too much economy here and the flow will be insufficient to supply two points at the same time, thus the unfortunate in the shower suddenly gets frozen or steam cleaned when a hot or cold tap is turned on elsewhere.

Reducing the sizes is not necessarily done with the intention of being dishonest. It may just be assumed you want the job done as cheaply as possible. Although the end product will work, after a fashion, a little more money spent on it at the time would have made it more efficient. It might be that the tradesmen, having given a quote, will then economize on materials to increase his profit. Either way you run the risk of getting scalded, so it pays to know a little about it.

It is worth repeating that only bills from bona fide registered tradesmen are acceptable for deduction against Capital Gains Tax, or for claiming a grant. A well established artisan is also more likely to be still around to honour a guarantee in the event of future problems. In any case it will be necessary to produce the bills.

Obviously there are risks involved in having a stranger working in your house, especially if you are not able to be there a lot of the time. On the whole I have found that French workmen are meticulously honest. From time to time though they have to employ labour which might not always be so reliable. They can't be there to supervise all the time, especially when the need arises to go and get materials, the lack of which might be holding up the job. To minimize the risk it is wise to keep the place as empty of your personal effects as possible until the job is complete. Apart from anything else, empty rooms are the easiest to work in. Time spent clambering around or moving things can frustrate a workman to the extent that the job might suffer.

It is hard to imagine the amount of dust caused by renovating old buildings. It gets everywhere, no matter what precautions are taken to prevent it. Electronic equipment such as computers, tape recorders and radios are especially vulnerable and should be really well protected. With this in mind, never throw away large polythene sheets. The type that a mattress is packed in is ideal for dust protection.

As a final word on tradesmen, there are often those who like to work on or even specialize in old property. Others may only have experience in the building of new homes and so will be less likely to understand the reasons and so not know the cure for leaks, cracks and so on. Even if it takes longer, it is advisable to find someone familiar with your kind of property and all its inherent problems, and who has an interest in restoration.

They still believe in apprenticeships in France, so the chances are that you will have a good job done by a skilled craftsman who takes a pride in his work. All major work will carry a ten-year guarantee, and minor items are covered for two years.

Although there is a tendency towards builders from the UK moving in to some of the regions popular with the Brits, such as the Dordogne (they advertise in the local and 'English' papers there) they will lack some of the advantages of the French tradesmen, who will know exactly where to find all materials and be familiar with their often different characteristics. A few weeks with them also has the advantage of improving your French no end. Using local men can help your dealings with the *mairie* as well as they are more likely to know all the rules and regulations. This is not to knock British builders, some of whom are well established and obviously good at their work. Some, however, tend to regard it as a bit of a holiday in the sun before they find out just how exhausting working in the sun can be.

5   Order of Work

The actual starting point of the work is bound to depend on the state of the property, but fair or dilapidated, it is always an awe inspiring moment when the long-winded process of buying is finally completed and the title is in your name. You will then realize the enormity of the task you have taken on and wonder where on earth to start.

It is a sensation not unlike shock which is tinged with a fair measure of excitement – the former caused by sudden doubts as to your ability to see it all through (and even your audacity at having entered on the project in the first place) and the latter by the realization that the finished article will be a creation of your own imagination and maybe your own hands as well.

These emotions, whilst gazing at the scene of your future endeavours are quite likely to delay the actual moment of starting work, but whether it be tens or hundreds of hours confronting you, whether you are going to do it yourself or organize others to do it for you, it is very important to have a system. Attacking the task erratically will end up costing time and money.

The following plan of action will no doubt need modifying to suit individual cases because not everyone will be starting with a ruin. For those who are, however, the basic idea is to start at the top and work downwards with the intention of weather-proofing and making good. By this method the interior work will not be interrupted or damaged by rain or snow.

The planning of the work can never start too soon as there are so many things to think of. Unless you are a trained architect or builder it is quite easy, in your eagerness to get on with the job, to overlook things like wiring. It would be very frustrating, for example, to finish pointing, rendering and plastering an internal wall only to have to start hacking channels to wire up light switches and power points. Hence the electrician and plumber as well should be called in at an early stage so that their conduits and piping can be in place before the plasterer does his thing. In both cases their part in the operation will have to be staggered to fit in with the other work.

As it is very likely that all these tradesmen will be self employed and work individually rather than for a firm, this often calls for the skill and application of an army general to get the logistics right. There is no doubt that the person doing the whole thing themselves has the advantage, because they can fit in each task as required, and if they have planned it well the right materials will be on hand at the right time. Planning for others is never easy, and it will lower the co-ordinator's blood pressure if it is taken as inevitable that some jobs will be held up whilst waiting for one of those involved to finish a job elsewhere and get back to yours.

You will also need to be very firm and clear in communicating exactly what you want. The electrician, for example, left to work without detailed instructions, will probably give you one power point per room. In France it is quite common to see extension leads and mobile sockets trailing around the floor of the average sitting room. We have already mentioned what the plumber might do! Detailed sketches and written specifications, especially where there is a language problem, will help each tradesman to know what you want and where you want it. He will then probably tell you why it is impossible, impractical or inadvisable for various reasons. Dogged persistance usually wins through in the end though. This contrary attitude adopted by some tradesmen is often well intentioned and angled towards economy. Some just can't see, for example, why anyone should want more than one power point to a room.

By the same token an individual tradesman might try to get you to change the order of work because he can see a more logical course. It pays to listen, because he might be right. You should be aware, however, that his suggestion might be entirely for his own convenience because he wants to finish his part and get off to another job. As a result this could mess up your carefully conceived plan and pose future problems. It might, on the other hand, be because his brother, who is a farmer, has a tractor and trailer which can shift all the rubble and other material destined for the local tip, but it won't be available for a few days. Clearly some flexibility will be necessary from time to time.

Bearing this sort of thing in mind, the work should proceed roughly as follows:

1. Insurance

Make sure that you have insurance to cover the building work and any accidents that might result from it, including personal injury and injuries to third parties. Also make sure that the necessary safety equipment – masks, goggles, gloves, helmets etc. – are on hand.

2. Rubbish

Clear away all unwanted material to the local tip. This will not only give good, clean working space, but also allow a more detailed survey of the building than was previously possible. Do not throw away anything that might be of use later on such as stones from demolished walls and restorable windows and doors. (There is nothing like the real thing to look authentic.) Doors you do not intend to use again, but which are sound, make good scaffold planks. Keep all whole roof tiles. Don't be in a hurry to discard fallen beams. Even if the ends are rotten they can be cut off, treated and used in a garage or over a fireplace. Keep any other useful lengths of timber if sound, and so on. The message is: don't be hasty. However tempting it may be to get rid of everything in sight and make a clean start, a lot of these things will have to be bought new or diligently searched for later on.

3. Supports

Support anything that appears to be in a dangerous state such as beams, joists, window and door lintels, loose wall stones and chimneys using well placed extending props, wedges, lengths of timber etc. General demolition of old rendering and so on can cause considerable vibration, which in turn can disturb other things. Where such work is taking place in an apartment that isn't on the top floor, supporting the beams and joists holding up the ceiling is especially important. Where the ends have deteriorated the rendering and plaster might be all that is holding them in place and hasty removal will allow them to settle if not fall. A movement of even half an inch is enough to create cracks in the walls and floor tiles of the apartment above, and could become the first claim on your insurance.

4. The Roof
In extreme cases, where beams and joists have rotted, the tiles will have to be removed and carefully stored while the necessary timbers are replaced. Where the main beams are sound, which is quite common as some last centuries, but the smaller timbers are cracked (longitudinal cracks are usually not a problem) or sagging, these can be replaced or doubled up as necessary. Whilst all the timbers are exposed from the top, take this rare opportunity to treat them generously with a good brand of preservative containing a rot inhibitor and worm killer. This can be done by brush from the top, but when the timbers are not exposed and it is necessary to work from underneath, a garden spray with a pump makes for better penetration. (Wear mask and goggles as the mist is toxic and cover tiles below, especially terracotta which can stain permanently.) Replace all cracked tiles. Make good all chimneys, chimney pots and flashings. If you are intending to install TV, have the aerial fitted at this stage while ladders and scaffolding are in place. It will be cheaper than later on.

5. Gutters
Unblock, repair or replace gutters and downpipes. Take special care when dismantling ceramic gutters and pipes, which break easily and are becoming hard to replace. Some old buildings in the south or other drier regions have no gutters. Where the overhangs are sufficient to protect the wall, this is a matter of choice, but in some cases lack of guttering may be the cause of damp walls or complaints from neighbours with a lower roof taking all your spillage. In either case the fitting of gutters might be advisable and is best done while all the scaffolding for the roof repairs is in place.

6. Walls

Remove all cracked or loose rendering. If unsure, tap with a hammer – loose rendering will sound hollow. This might have to be a total removal job, or just a question of patching where the majority is sound. If in doubt, remove. In stone or brick buildings check the mortar. If it has gone soft and powdery, rake out and repoint. Do the same if it is damp and soft, but check out the reason why and cure it. (This might have already been cured in the course of roof and gutter repair.)

7. Windows and Doors

Remove, restore or replace as necessary. If you managed to save any old glass which can be cut down to size, you should use this as it will look more authentic. New glass can look too perfect. Where shutters play a major part in keeping out the weather these should also be replaced or repaired at this stage and the woodwork of each item carefully treated and painted for survival against the climatic extremes.

8. Foundations

Where subsidence is evident, and shown up by cracks in the walls and sagging or cracked lintels etc., the foundations may be in need of underpinning. Diagnoses and subsequent work is the province of the specialist. An architect can advise on this. Problems of rising damp often mean that the earth has to be moved away from the foundations to insert a plastic membrane, or a silicone injected damp course. (Few old buildings have a damp course.) It can also be caused by blocked drains, down pipes, or old drainage channels which have cracked.

9. Internal Demolition

Hack off all loose rendering and plaster. Rake out all decayed mortar. (This operation frequently loosens stones which will subsequently fall out if not propped up or wedged in place until repointing secures them.) Rotten and badly cracked plaster on the ceilings should also be removed at this stage, plus non-restorable staircases and internal dividing walls where opening up of rooms is planned. (Check if walls are supporting walls before removal. If they are, extending props will be needed until lintels or beams are installed to replace them.) After all the demolition is done (or when you are short of space) remove all waste material to the tip.

Install all necessary wiring in approved conduits. Piping for water delivery should also run through a PVC conduit, if the plan is to embed it in a new concrete floor. This gives room for expansion and contraction. The piping should also be lagged if it will be vulnerable to the cold. Install all necessary PVC drainage pipes. Where the ends of any pipes are to be left open until later connection, block them against falling dust and rubble.

10. Floors
Install new floors as necessary. If reinforced concrete, leave any intended ceramic tiling until last. If wood, protect very carefully.

11. Walls
Repoint, render and plaster as necessary.

12. Ceilings
Having first completed wiring and pipe runs, install insulation and lining board. Tape up ready for decorating.

13. Internal Dividing Walls
Erect to form bathroom, kitchen, etc. Plaster or line as necessary, having made provision for light-switch wiring, and for embedding edge of bath, shower tray etc.

14. New Staircases
Installing these now will make it easier to carry materials to upper floors, but if in timber, be meticulous about protecting the treads. Hardboard or thick cardboard is useful here.

15. Installation of Bathroom
Protect all bathroom equipment against decorating damage.

16. Installation of Kitchen
Including completion of all plumbing, electric water heating, etc.

17. Decorating Throughout

18. Finishing of Electrics
Attaching switches, wall sockets, lights, etc.

19. Tiling
Including floor tiling as necessary and kitchen and bathroom wall tiling.

As you will see, this list can be taken as a general guide only. If it is your intention to install central heating, sophisticated alarm systems, new fireplaces and chimneys, balconies, roof terraces, window grills in cast iron, etc., they will all have to be fitted into a logical slot in the overall operation. Work will have to be tailored to individual requirements and also around the availability of tradesmen. There are two main requirements: to work towards weather-proofing and to plan ahead in order to avoid the need to demolish finished surfaces or items because something was forgotten earlier.

If you can take advantage of the seasons, so much the better. If the work is starting in the winter, for example, a leaky roof might be best covered with a heavy duty tarpaulin and repairs left until the weather is better.

It will be noticed, during the work, that a staggering amount of rubble is produced from even quite minor demolition jobs, so removal will be a fairly regular operation. Work carries on a lot better in clean, uncluttered surroundings.

6 Buying Materials

Most tradesmen will look after this aspect of the job themselves, thus depriving a lot of owners of the experience of searching out obscure items of plumbing, electrical gear, or whatever from the nearest supplier. Some will be doing it themselves, however, and others, who are not, will see the advantage in collecting a missing item rather than have the job held up while the worker goes out shopping.

In the main, experience has shown that the most economical way to buy materials is to go to one of the large national superstores. Not only are the prices reasonable, but the chances are that most of what you want is available under one roof, which saves time. (Useful suppliers' names appear at the back of the book.)

Having said this, you might be lucky and find that a local village hardware shop (*quincaillerie*) sells a range of plumbing and electrical fittings at a reasonable price. If you explain that you are renovating a house nearby and will need to buy a lot, but not necessarily all at once, an enterprising shopkeeper will give you a discount and, very likely, a credit account as well. This will bring his prices more in line with the large superstores, so as the latter may be several miles away it could sometimes be more economical to shop locally.

All the large stores have promotions from time to time, with such items as bathroom and kitchen equipment being put on special offer. Large savings can be made if your budget allows you to buy at these times. Needless to say, these offers never seem to crop up exactly when they are wanted. So, if they include such items as bath, bidet, sink, w.c. hot water tank etc., secure storage is necessary until they are installed. They are all items which are especially vulnerable to damage. To save space, a lot of things can be stored in a bath, including the legs if they have been detached. If the bath is cast iron, however, wrap up the legs well or they will eventually stain the enamel coating on the bath.

Another advantage of the large store is that many have an advisory service. This can consist of a specialist in each department, or in some cases a series of leaflets (*fiche conseil*) with instructions on how to use most materials.

Tool hire is now a regular feature of most stores, including such items as scaffolding, ladders, cement mixers, static generators and other things you will normally not want to keep permanently. Smaller tools such as sanders, circular saws, drills, wallpaper strippers, etc., are also available. Short term hire tends to be expensive though. An afternoon of say four hours frequently costs nearly half of the charge for a whole weekend. So careful planning is vital, not only to make sure the whole job can be completed within the hire time, with help laid on if necessary, but also that all the materials are bought in advance (especially if the hire is over a weekend) to save the aggravation of running out just after closing time on Saturday.

If there is more than one large store in your area (which seems to be the trend) it pays to shop around. Expensive items like copper piping or electric wiring, for which vast lengths can be consumed in the course of a new installation, can vary considerably in price. As with most things, bulk buying is always the most economical, so careful calculation cuts costs.

Some large stores are specialists and some stock practically everything, but naturally the specialists can keep a wider range of their goods, making it more likely that you can find exactly what you want. Castorama, Mr Bricolage and others keep a limited range of most things, whereas Lapeyre specialize in wooden items such as doors, staircases, windows, shutters, cupboards, etc., in vast quantities and good quality. Brosette carry a stock of plumbing fittings so huge that you are almost certain to find what you are looking for. MBM (in the south and west) or Gedimat nationally are best for general building materials such as cement, plaster, bricks, tiles, timber, etc., and as they cater for the building trade generally, they are usually happy to arrange a discount for regular buyers.

Anyone renovating a ruin will use vast quantities of sand. Although this can be bought in plastic bags at most large DIY stores, it is infinitely cheaper to go and find the local *sablier* and buy it loose. Most have a weighbridge, so if you fill up a trailor this will have to be weighed before and after. If you are only filling up ten or twenty bucketfuls they will usually charge a set price, say 10 francs a time. This sort of sand is usually very coarse, and so will need sieving for some jobs, but it is usually washed and so otherwise ready to use.

The main thing to know when pricing up material is the difference between HT (*hors tax*) and TTC (*tout tax compris*). Only the latter will tell you what you are actually going to pay, including VAT (TVA in France) and any other additions. When asking prices, it is very common to be quoted the former and the unpleasant surprise comes later at the cash desk when it is embarrassing, with a queue of impatient shoppers breathing down your neck, to back out.

Check-out operators are sometimes careless about handing you the till receipt, so it pays to make a habit of asking for it. They will also supply a proper receipt (*reçu* or *facture*) on demand.

Payment
UK credit cards such as Access and Visa are widely accepted in France these days, but you may be asked to provide identification. Over a certain sum, usually 1,000 francs (about £100) two forms of identification might be asked for, e.g. passport and driving licence.

Delivery
A lot of the large DIY stores now operate a short term van hire for customers, with prices that are very competitive and can vary according to the amount you are spending. This can be very useful for the large or heavy items where it is best to put the strain on commercial suspension, which is designed to bear this sort of weight, rather than risk damage by overloading your own vehicle.

Buying Second-hand
There are numerous ways to find second-hand items, e.g. the free advertising papers to be found on the counters of bread

and other shops, *petites annonces* which are postcard-size
private ads to be found on boards near supermarket
check-outs as part of a free service for customers. Also, in
recent years, shops specifically selling used equipment of all
types have opened up in many places. These are usually called
a *dépôt de vente* (sale-room).

It pays, before buying second-hand, to compare these
prices with those of new items in a shop, if possible. Often the
prices are not that different on some things, especially
furniture, and the used ones come without a guarantee.
Stainless steel sink units, however, can often be found quite
cheaply second-hand.

Treasures on the Tip
The *décharge public* is sometimes rich in useful items. Large
demolition companies seldom restore old doors and windows
etc. It is quicker for them to dump them and buy new. A lot
of these will not only be in restorable condition, but also in
authentic styles. They can often be made to fit the required
aperture. A lot of tips will have a notice saying *recuperation
interdit* (recovery not allowed) but no one seems to take any
notice. In fact, whole families seem to be in regular
attendance there, pouncing on any arriving vehicle to see if
there is anything valuable amongst the rubbish. Their interest
is mostly in scrap metals of various types, so you won't make
enemies by taking old woodwork or sheets of polystyrene for
insulation or plastic paint buckets to contain your next load
of rubbish etc. Sometimes it is hard to tear yourself away!

7   The Roof

The roofs (*toiture*) on properties in France can be divided
into several different styles which have developed according
to the regional climate. Where rainfall is common and snow
can be expected in the winter, roofs are steeper to encourage
rapid drainage and the roof covering (i.e. the tiles) will fit
tightly together offering little chance for rain to seep through.
In parts of the north, the wall facing the prevailing weather is
often also covered with slates or flat tiles to save frequent
saturation causing internal dampness.

In the south, where the climate is much drier, most roofs
are covered with the semi-conical pan tile (*tuile canal*) and
the roof angle is much less acute – often as little as
twenty-five degrees. As the name suggests, the drainage is still
good, but the old pan tiles are much less of an engineered fit,
thus leaving plenty of room for air to circulate and help keep
the supporting timbers in good condition. Before the internal
lining is fitted, anyone inside who is high enough up to look
down the angle of the ceiling might be alarmed to see daylight
coming through various gaps. This is quite normal, however,
and not a problem if there is sufficient overlap. Unlike slates
or flat tiles where the overlap is governed by the battens
underneath that they are nailed into or hooked over, pan tiles
are not fixed; each one merely rests on the one beneath. The
overlap should be at least a quarter of the length on the tile in
order to keep out wind-driven rain.

The tile regions are roughly as follows:

Brittany, Normandy, Anjou   slate (*ardois*)
Paris, Bourgogne and the centre   flat terracotta tiles
North, Pyrenees and parts of   (*tuile plate terre cuite*)
   the centre   fish scale slate
                (*en écaille de poisson terre cuite*)
South and west   pan tiles (*tuile en canal*)

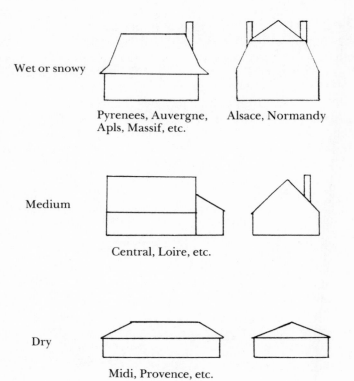

Wet or snowy

Pyrenees, Auvergne,   Alsace, Normandy
Apls, Massif, etc.

Medium

Central, Loire, etc.

Dry

Midi, Provence, etc.

There are, of course, small variations where builders have adopted the style of another region for personal preference and where, in some of the mountain areas of the Ardèche and Auvergne, a local, very thick, rough slate is used known as *lauzes* or *pans brisés*. Also, these zones only apply to the older buildings. In the last sixty or seventy years much use has been made in all regions of the more sophisticated *tuile mécanique*, the moulded shape of which gives better protection against the elements than the older styles.

Where slates or flat tiles were used, these were often cut or moulded differently in parts of the north, centre and Pyrenees with the lower end of the tile coming to a point angled at forty-five degrees (see diagram). This forms the distinctive fish scale pattern when laid and gives the impression that the tiles are laid in rows at an angle of forty-five degrees from the gutter rather than vertically up and down the roof.

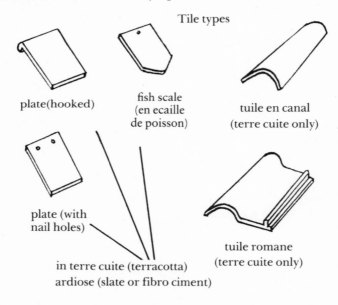

Tile types

plate(hooked)

fish scale
(en ecaille
de poisson)

tuile en canal
(terre cuite only)

plate (with
nail holes)

in terre cuite (terracotta)
ardiose (slate or fibro ciment)

tuile romane
(terre cuite only)

In some of the regions the edging and ridge tiles are often very decorative. Like fancy brickwork, there was a time when all the various elements of a house were made to look distinctive and artistic instead of just being conveniently weather-proof living units. The ridge tiles should always be overlapped to give protection from the prevailing wind and rain, so if the mortar cracks eventually there is less likelihood of leaks.

Each roof tile type has its own particular way of being affixed (see diagrams) and therefore a different type of base to fix to. On steep roofs, tiles are either hooked over battens or nailed into them, whereas pan tiles are just laid on a flat surface (planks or slabs of *terre cuite* known as *parefeuilles* which lie across the rafters).

Elements of a Pan Tile Roof

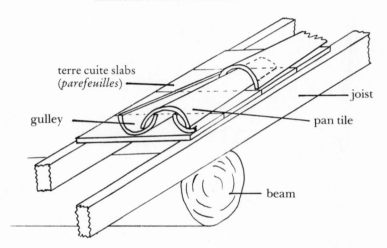

The weight of each successive tile is sufficient to hold the next in place. As mentioned previously, the overlap is important, so if a row of newly laid tiles is found to be slightly short at the ridge it is better to include another tile and increase the overlap slightly all the way down rather than gaining the extra length by decreasing it.

France is proud of her regional roof styles and in most areas would prefer them to be kept traditional when restoring. Fortunately most buyers of old property these days are attracted by the historic interest and would not wish to deviate from the original. In years gone by, however, when the preservation of interesting architecture was often ignored, apart from buildings of national importance, much use was

Roof Tiles

Tuiles Plates

prevailing wind

mortar

Ardoise

fixing by crochets

fixing by nails

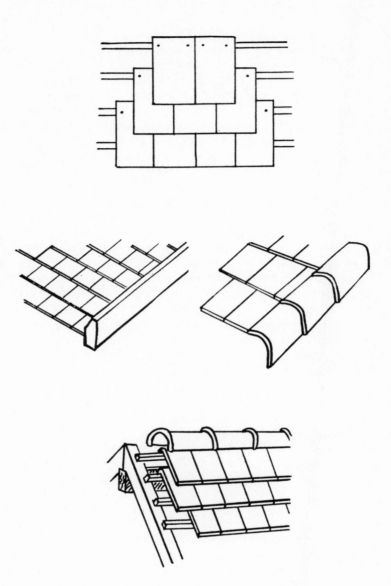

made of such materials as corrugated sheeting, making for some rather unpleasant blots on otherwise attractive 'roofscapes'.

A major roof restoration job might call for the services of a traditional tiler. As with thatchers, these skilled artisans are becoming a rare species. Try consulting the *mairie*, or the preservation society attached to it (if there is one) or a local architect.

In the pan tile regions there are corrugated sheetings which form a compromise. Often known as 'canalite' or a similar trade name, the intention is to form a watertight roof, the ridges then being covered with pan tiles merely for decoration. At a quick glance the roof looks reasonably authentic, especially where there is guttering to conceal the lack of gulley tiles. This sort of panel always used to be made from asbestos but are now known as *fibrociment*.

Personally I see little point in the use of these panels rather than to do a quick, cheap job. They are far from problem free, being liable to split if screwed down too tight. The screw-bolts have a rubber collar, but these do not always form a good seal, giving the temptation to overtighten and where the supporting timber is not true (and wood seldom is) the panel will distort and be prone to splitting. Once the pan tiles have been laid up and down the ridges, the heads of the screw-bolts become concealed, so anyone trying to do a roof repair who stands on a tile with a bolt head under it will crack the tile. Possibly the only dubious advantage is that the roof is lighter, having only half the usual quantity of pan tiles and therefore doesn't need such heavy timbers to support it. Even this is nullified, however, where the intention was to expose the beams to the room below as a feature of the decor. The real thing not only looks better, but is adequately weatherproof if properly done and will, if you have had it restored or repaired, carry a ten-year guarantee from the builder.

It will be hoped, of course, that the roof of your property is sound, or at worst just in need of minor repairs. This will depend not only on the condition and sufficiency of the tiles, but also on the supporting timbers. These will vary in shape and size depending on the region. In the pan tile zones there will be two or three massive horizontal beams evenly spaced between gutter and ridge and running from wall to wall except where the roof slopes down to all four sides of the building, there will be an even larger beam down each sloping ridge support the horizontal beams. Smaller timbers (around 7cm x 7cm) are then laid vertically (from gutter to ridge) at 40cm centres to accommodate the *terre cuite* slabs (or the modern 40cm x 20cm x 25mm honeycomb brick) on which the pan tiles are laid in ridges and gulleys, with the wide end downwards for the ridges and narrow end for the gulleys. Ridges, edge tiles (and sometimes the bottom row) are cemented with mortar.

Flashings for chimneys and where the roof juts over a wall are more or less the same as those in the UK. They are available in rigid zinc or flexible aluminium/bitumen material which can be bought in rolls in various widths. The latter are heated with a blowlamp for adhesion, and a special bitumen primer is usually painted on first.

In other zones the roof timbers tend to be more like those in the UK – lighter and pre-formed into the profile of the roof and lined with waterproof sheets of roofing felt or similar material, before the battens are attached horizontally and the tiles affixed to them.

Where a large beam needs replacing it is likely to be a job for a mobile crane, as they are often of 45cm square, or more, in section and several metres in length. This can become a problem in town or village centre property where the streets are often too narrow for the crane to approach. In some instances, a crane with a long jib might be able to do the job from the next street if it is wider and reaching over the intervening rooftops. (Make sure the company is adequately insured where the property of others is at risk.) This will mean the hire of a larger crane as the lifting capability decreases proportionately the further away the object to be lifted happens to be. There are certain fork-lift trucks around designed for high lifting, but there will either have to be an entrance large enough to get one inside the building, or blocks and tackles and/or much manpower will be needed to haul the beam up into place as it reaches the top of the outer wall. It would probably be safer to hire a tower crane as these can be built on site in confined spaces.

The builder should be able to organize or advise on the

availability of plant equipment in the locality, but those doing the job themselves will have to search around the local *zone industriel* where such things are often to be found.

When all else fails there are two other possibilities: moulding a steel-reinforced concrete lintel *in situ*, by forming suitable shuttering (a plywood trough the concrete will be poured into around the lengths of steel rod), or you can laminate a beam by gluing together several planks until the required thickness is achieved. Provided that the sides of the planks are well smoothed to fit snugly, good quality glue is used and well clamped or screwed tight during the period of cure, the end result will be a very strong, rigid beam every bit as good as the original. Suitably planed and stained with the corners chamfered, it will also appear authentic unless closely scrutinized. It is also possible to form a hollow down the centre in the process which is large enough to accept a wiring conduit for lighting, if required.

A lot of old roofs have a visible amount of sag, which can be caused by a gradual distortion of the beams caused by the weight of the roof over many years, or by cracked, broken or rotten timbers. The former is not a problem unless the sag is pronounced enough to indicate a definite weakness. Being very small in relation to the area of the roof, the tiles are able to mould themselves around gentle undulations and remain weather-proof. Geometric perfection should not be expected in an old building where irregularities are a part of the charm. In the latter case the timbers will have to be replaced or doubled up as necessary. When in doubt, consult an experienced, traditional roof repairer or an architect.

A glance through the catalogues of the large supply stores will show that all types of tiles are still available in the original materials. Inevitably, modern methods of manufacture make them look a little too perfect, so it takes a few years of weathering and a healthy growth of roof moss before they start to look right. Slates are blacker and more shiny than pan tiles which are thinner, more consistent in colour and moulded shape. The latter look better if interspersed with the old tiles rather than being all in one patch. This is quite easy to do when only the top and bottom are fixed.

Seekers after authenticity, if they are prepared to search and not in too much of a hurry (understandably this may not apply to those already having to put out buckets to catch the drips) will usually be able to find old tiles. Ask around the demolition companies – the odd, enterprising one will not only keep these, but also, if they have storage space, they often have old beams, decorative chimney pots, doors, shutters and even old wooden staircases, either straight or spiral type. Normally they will only keep the restorable items, which will probably mean a little work, but the end result will be worth it.

Those wishing to do their own roof repairs would do well to consult the nearest library. Most have a good selection of books on traditional buildings and architecture, showing many of the techniques in illustrated form, so even those without much French will find these a great help. French libraries normally allow everyone to consult their reference works, but any home owner who wishes to take books home to study can become a member. The usual demands are a passport, proof of payment of a bill such as rates or electricity and a one time only payment of around £5.

When converting a loft into a proper room, the addition of a roof window is a good thing to consider, not only as a means of letting in light, but also to give safe access to the roof without the need for ladders or scaffolding. This can be invaluable for minor repairs, erecting TV aerials and so on. Needless to say, a roof ladder with a hook which fastens over the ridge will still be necessary on steep, flat tiled roofs, both for the protection of the tiles and the safety of the repairer. Southern, pan tiles roofs can be walked on with care, but wear soft shoes and spread your weight over two tiles at a time (ridge to ridge) to avoid cracking. Inevitably some will suffer so a few spares are always useful.

Roof Problem Check-list
The following can all cause leaks:

1. Cracked ridge tiles or degraded mortar
2. Cracked or missing roof tiles. (Tiles can crack with age, or by falling masonry from a chimney or neighbouring roof. Slates especially can slide off when the fixing nails eventually rust away.)
3. Broken or degraded flashing around chimneys or where the tiles meet a wall

4. Uncapped chimneys which are out of use
5. Chimneys with inadequate rain protection (see diagram)
6. Rendered chimneys where the rendering has cracked
7. Blocked or damaged gulleys in between gables
8. Blocked gutters and downpipes
9. Cracked edge tiles or degraded mortar
10. Broken or missing weather board (where used instead of edge tiles)
11. Failure of internal support causing too much sag
12. Cracked roofing panels (where used)
13. Damaged roofing felt
14. Insufficient tile overlap
15. Tile creep. (This applies mostly to pan tiles which tend to slide downwards over a period until there is no overlap to keep out the rain. Can be caused by building work vibration, cats walking on the roof, very close thunderclaps and high winds. The cure is merely to slide the tile back up into place.)

8 Walls and Appendages to the Main Structure

It would be very unusual to find an old building with perfect walls (*murs*); durable though most of them are, they more often than not show some evidence of advancing age and consistent attack by the climate which leads to expansion and contraction and earth movements, however miniscule. In fact, it is a long-term struggle that time eventually wins.

One often hears optimistic comments like 'it has already been standing for over two hundred years and probably will go on for another hundred.' In a lot of cases it will too, but with a little help along the way that life expectancy could be doubled.

To a certain extent, a buyer of old property, especially one in a run down state, needs to be optimistic to face the work ahead of him in a positive manner that will restore a depressing, dilapidated ruin into a dignified, attractive home.

The type of brick or stone used for the building of walls will depend on the age and the region. The thing they both have in common is that they are joined by mortar, which deteriorates over a long period and reverts to powder. If nothing is done to arrest this process, a combination of rain, wind and gravity will remove the mortar to the extent that the wall will become vulnerable to collapse if nothing is done.

The repair procedure, known in the UK as repointing (a pointed trowel is used to force in the new mortar) is simple, but very labour intensive and extremely important. Apart from a major failure of the structure being possible, decayed mortar can also be a source of leaks and a means of transmitting dampness through the wall.

In a lot of old buildings repointing will have to be done on both the external and internal face of the wall to restore its strength sufficiently. After all, in the course of general repairs and alterations the walls are going to be subject to a lot of strain, especially from the vibration caused by opening up holes for drainage or wiring conduits, water piping, location points for new joists, removal and replacement of cracked lintels, new openings or enlargement of existing windows and so on. One way or another they are going to take a lot of punishment and should be made as strong as possible to cope with this.

Vertical and horizontal cracks should be treated in the same way as the other joints between the stone or brickwork, but the reason for their existence should also be found and cured (see check-list).

As repointing is time consuming but simple it is the sort of job that quite a few owners like to do themselves. This is because the end result, where the stones or bricks are to be left exposed, can be very satisfactory and because long jobs cost money which could be better spent on more specialized tasks where skilled help is necessary.

The first requirement is a dust mask, especially when working inside. The dust produced is bad enough on its own for the lungs, throat, eyes, ears and so on, but it also contains lime and, in the case of old chimney breasts, fine soot as well. Personal protection is therefore very important. Safety goggles can help if they are a tight fit, otherwise the resulting dust and grit will have to be flushed out afterwards with an eye bath.

The aim is to rake out all the loose mortar for replacement later. This means anything that can be coaxed out with a suitable tool (e.g. a thin, sharp trowel, old screwdriver, small stone chisel or pointed hammer.)

Very thick stone walls are often built in two layers, the intervening space filled with mortar, clay, grit or any old rubble that happened to be handy at the time, or that is how it seems two or three hundred years later after it has dried out and turned to powder. By no means are all the stones forming the wall flat top and bottom, so in the course of raking out the old mortar it is quite common for a stone to slide out, followed by a small landslide issuing from the cavity. The only way to stop this is to plug the hole, preferably with the stone that fell out and wedge it back in place somehow (maybe lean a piece of timber against it). If a stone above can be conveniently removed and if the centre filling there happens to be firmer, wet mortar can be poured in to fill up the space (not too wet, or it will run out of the gaps). If not, keep forcing mortar in when repointing, until it will accept no more. It is a very long, dusty job, and will do your knuckles and fingernails no good at all.

Because gravity is seldom an ally, mortar for repointing has to be just the right consistency; too wet and it will run out as you try to push it in; too dry and it will crumble and then fall out. Some advise using a squirt or two of washing up liquid in the mix to make it more plastic, which can work with rendering too. Practice will be necessary to get it right, and there will be plenty of that.

One thing that will help is to wash out the gaps before starting to apply the new mortar. When the stonework is wet it doesn't absorb all the water out of the mortar and thus make it difficult to adhere. A garden spray with a pump is useful here, or even a small hand flower spray. Outside, the wall can be hosed down, provided the stones are firm and unlikely to be dislodged by the jet.

Internally, thought should be given to wiring runs for switches and power points. These can be wedged in place, often weaving a tortuous path around the stones, following the largest gaps, before the repointing starts. (Refer to section on electrics for circuit data.)

The mortar mix will often depend on the colour of the stones; if five (of sand) to one (of cement) is used, the result will be a sandy grey. Six to one will make it a shade lighter. Whiter sand than the normal builders' sand can be found in some places. If, however, your requirement is for a really white joint it will be necessary to use Chaux, a lime product available at builders' merchants. A typical mix would be six parts of Chaux, one part of cement and eighteen parts of sand. More Chaux and less sand will make the mix whiter still but progressively weaker.

The actual technique of filling the gaps can be achieved in many different ways. The French tend to flick it from the trowel, by which process the mortar enters the gaps at speed. (They render in the same way.) Quite a bit of practice is needed for this method and if your aim is out you are faced with a major cleaning job. If the wall is to be subsequently rendered, this won't matter, but where the stonework is to be left exposed, care is needed if it is to end up looking good. A slim trowel can be useful for pressing in the new mortar, but like any sand and cement mix, too much pressing will make it collapse as the water content is squeezed out. Sometimes it is better to press it in once and then leave it to stiffen up for an hour or two (depending on the temperature) before returning to finish it. You can be working on other areas in the meantime. Some find it easier to wear heavy gardening gloves and literally push it in with their fingers, or use a blunt piece of wood as a ram. Only practice will prove which method works best for you.

As pointing is such a slow process, mortar should be made up in small quantities, especially in hot weather, to avoid wastage. Start with half a bucketful at first, and if you have to stop for an hour or so, cover the bucket with a wet cloth.

However expert you become, a certain amount will inevitably end up on the floor, so if this is tiled, timbered or in any other way worth preserving, protect it with hardboard or cardboard before starting work and the final cleaning up will be quicker.

Where an internal stone wall is very irregular, and would not end up looking very good if left exposed, it is quite common practice to build up an inner wall of 50mm honeycomb 40cm x 20cm bricks. This will provide a nice, flat surface for plastering (see section on internal walls). Alternatively, you can dry line the walls with plasterboard. Both methods are acceptable if a clean flat surface is required, and both have the additional advantage of concealing wiring and piping runs, but on no account should either of these methods be used merely to hide the horrors underneath, the wall should still be repointed and thus strengthened first where necessary.

Rendering

When the repointing and cleaning up is complete, the next job may be to render the wall with a cement mix which is normally five or six parts sand to one of cement. The aim is to provide a strong, flat surface suitable to be skimmed with plaster.

This is not a job for the faint-hearted, or for anyone with a weak heart for that matter, as it is extremely heavy work and in most cases best left to the professional. The art of getting rendering to stick to the wall is too complex a subject to be covered here, but there are a few ways the untrained enthusiast can succeed. One of these, as with all things, is practice, preferably having watched a professional first. Once again, the French artisans throw it on the wall using a fairly large trowel which propels it with considerable force until the depth and state of cure is suitable for rubbing it flat with a wooden or plastic float. This method does the job well, but is wasteful of sand and cement, much of which ends up on the floor. Alternatively one can use the British method of spooning the mix on to the float and pressing it into the wall using upward strokes. (The float should never be steel, as used for plastering, but light plastic or wood) Never press too much in the same spot or it will lose adhesion and collapse as the water comes through to the surface.

Perhaps the easiest technique for the amateur is to use a form of shuttering. This is simply a matter of bracing (very firmly) a flat board against the area to be rendered, leaving a small gap between it and the stones (about 2.5cm) regulated by wedges, making sure the side edges are plugged (rolled up newspaper can be stuffed in) and pour in a runny mix of sand and cement. Twenty-four hours later (less in hot weather) the props and board can be removed, the board raised up on chocks until only the lower third of it remains on the area just done, wedges in place again and the process repeated until the top of the wall is reached.

By this method a good, sound, flat surface is achieved, provided care is taken to remove high spots along the top edge before repositioning. Don't be too ambitious. A door-sized board is quite sufficient and as the sand/cement/water mix is heavy, the bracing should be strong, and taken across to the opposite wall if possible. Also, the floor underneath should be clear and clean or covered with hardboard or similar so that should the board collapse through insufficient bracing the mixture can be recovered for another go.

Chipboard which is 19mm thick, suitably pre-sealed with varnish should be used, if no old, flat doors are available. If the sealing is adequate it can also be used for garage shelving or such like later.

Another advantage with this shuttering method is that the sand will not need sieving. Cheap builders' sand is usually quite coarse and will definitely need sieving if the rendering is to be floated on, as in the UK.

If you ask a French artisan the proportions of sand and cement used for rendering, it is quite likely he will say two to one. Now anyone knows that this would use up enormous and very costly quantities of cement for no good reason and make the finished job very brittle. Further enquiry will show that what he really meant was two *brouettes* of sand to one sack of cement. A *brouette* can either be a large wheelbarrow or the huge container grapes are put in by the pickers at harvest time prior to being unloaded into cart, trailer etc. Either type of container would result in a mix of around five or six to one.

Plastering

Like rendering, this is definitely an art and good plasterers are always in demand. A professional will probably tell you that the trick is to put water into the mixing trough, sprinkle the powder into it from a suitable trowel until it starts to settle on the surface, stop to smoke a cigarette, and then get it on the wall quickly. On no account stir it.

These instructions are quite sound. Stirring the powder into the water is inclined to make it cure too quickly, and the time taken to have a smoke (about five minutes?) allows the powder to thoroughly absorb the water. After this the mixture will harden quite quickly if left *en masse* in the trough or bucket (amateurs will find the latter sufficient to start with) and so no time should be wasted in spooning it on to a float with a flat trowel and spreading it on to the wall in upward strokes. Obviously practice makes one better at getting it flat first go, but if it goes on a bit lumpy all is not lost. There is a stage of cure between half an hour and an hour after application (depending on the temperature) when it has firmed up but not really hardened, when the edge of the steel float can be used as a scraper at right angles to the wall, to cut off the high spots. After a few firm strokes, downwards and across, the wall will begin to look flatter. Alternatively, one can wait until it is dry and rub it down with medium grade sandpaper wrapped around a piece of flat wood, or use an orbital sander, but this method creates more dust.

The next stage is to fill any troughs or imperfections, once the plaster is dry, with *enduit*, a cheaper but more efficient form of filler than some of the well-known brand names, and when dry, rub down smooth before painting.

A professional plasterer will do it quicker, at a price (in 1991 it cost between 35francs and 40francs per square metre). If you do it yourself, however, you can have the satisfaction of having done your own thing.

Plastering is largely a matter of timing, to get the mix right and then ensuring firm and confident application. The best way is to start small – half a bucketful spread on the wall is better than a large troughful, half of which goes off before you can use it. The harder it gets, the harder you have to press with the float to flatten it and the more tiring the job becomes. It is quite obvious when it reaches a state of cure and it is at this point which it should be thrown away.

Wall Check-list

1. *Cracks in external rendering or internal plaster*
   Not too important, but underlying cause might be. Investigate by removing any loose material. If found to be surface problem only, make good as appropriate.

2. *Horizontal cracks*
   Often found under windows and balconies. Frequently due to weakness in the floor at that level transmitting movement through the beams. Can sometimes be put right by supporting each beam in turn with an extending screw prop, raking out the decayed mortar where it enters the wall and renewing. If beam ends are softened – due to rot, check depth and extent. At worst the beam may have to be replaced, or saturated with rot inhibitor and supported further into the room where it is sound. This can be done individually by removal of the supporting stone and replacement with a stone that extends into the room (see diagram), or collectively by erecting a wall-to-wall lintel giving extra support to all the beams.

Better Support for a Beam with End Deteriorated

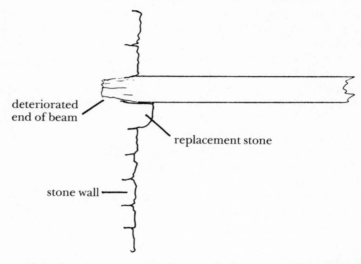

deteriorated
end of beam

replacement stone

stone wall

If the beam movement has made the external wall bulge outwards, it will be necessary to arrest this by installing one or more lengths of iron rod from one side of the building to the other (usually out of sight internally, i.e. below floor and above ceiling) attached to external ironwork, usually in the form of a cross.

3. *Vertical Cracks – low down*
   Caused by movement in foundations (if any). Small cracks are not important and will be cured in the repointing process. If the crack reappears or if it is large, underpinning might be necessary. Alternatively you might need to cure rising damp if that was what weakened the mortar. Consult an architect if in doubt.

4. *Vertical cracks – high up*
   Often the result of mortar decay caused by falling damp from a roof problem.
   If crack is wider at the top end it is usually caused by pressure from an internal beam or joist. This movement can be checked by installing iron rod as above.

5. *Rising damp*

There are numerous causes: development of surrounding land causing water to collect against wall or foundations, water from roof running into blocked or non-existent drainage.

Repair or install drainage system by inserting plastic membrane between damp soil and wall down to foundations and insert injected damp course or air-siphon tubes as advised.

6. *Damp patches on internal walls*

Check for old, porous, lead supply pipe from water mains. Replace with copper or polypropylene (25mm) as advised by plumber.

Can also be caused by old drainage channels running under house. You can verify this by lightly tapping your tiled floor. These channels (see diagram) are usually just covered by the floor tiles at the top. They often run from an outside toilet at the rear through to the main drain in the street near the front door in terraced property in a village or town. They are totally inadequate by today's standards with a potential leak at every joint. The cure is to remove the outside toilet and excavate until the

Old Style Stone Slab Drainage Channel with PVC Liner Inserted

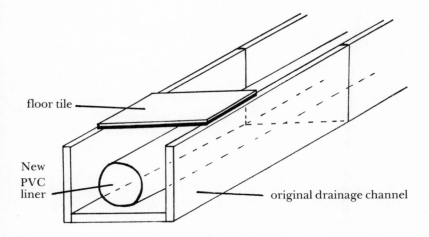

floor tile

New PVC liner

original drainage channel

drainage channel is exposed and insert 100mm PVC pipe which will then become the main drainage for the building (see drainage section). Rainwater falling on to corner buttresses can be the cause of internal dampness. The buttress should be well sealed into the wall.

7. *Midway damp patches on outside walls*

When it is obvious these are not caused by roof problems or rising damp from ground, check for leaks in supply or drainage pipes contained within wall. Once again it will be necessary to 'sound' the wall by tapping to find a vertical channel leading down to the main drainage.

Can also be caused by badly sealed shower tray spilling into wall.

None of these faults need to be regarded as potential catastrophies; they have probably been present in the property for a century or so. Consultation with an expert, careful scrutiny and planning for a long term repair is better than a panic job.

This also applies to wooden beams, which are amazingly durable. Frequently external softening or woodworm damage only affects the outer surface up to a depth of about half an inch, leaving the main strength of the beam intact. Thorough treatment with a brand of modern rot inhibitor and woodworm killer will check any further decay for years. Where the softening has a traceable cause, i.e. a leak in the wall, or lack of air circulation where covered by a false ceiling, this should be cured at the same time.

Appendages to the Main Structure
Chimneys
Whereas we tend to refer to a chimney as the actual smoke stack extending up from the roof, the French call the whole thing the *cheminée*, down to and including the fireplace, which they would only call the *foyer* when being technical (see diagram).

It is worth mentioning here that a working chimney must be swept every year as a legal requirement. This process, known as *ramonage* is carried out by a *ramoneur*, who issues a certificate each time it is done. Many insurance companies will not pay out on fire damage caused by a chimney without

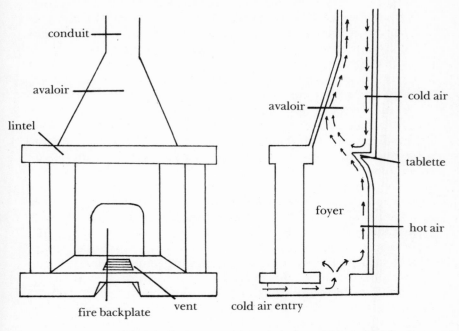

Typical Fireplace (bought whole or in kit form)

conduit

avaloir

lintel

fire backplate
vent

avaloir

foyer

cold air entry

cold air

tablette

hot air

a current certificate. It is not necessary for chimneys where the fireplace has been blocked off or where it is just used for ventilation, but it should be swept prior to blocking off to be on the safe side.

Although some chimney stacks are entirely external, being built on to an outer wall, most go up through the roof at some point, making for an interruption in the tiles and thus creating the need for various forms of flashings for weather-proofing. Because of this and the need for a smoke exit, old chimneys are a frequent source of leaks.

In these days of highly efficient coal or wood burning stoves it is normal for the smoke to be routed up through a rigid or flexible steel conduit, but where the smoke has been allowed to soak into the brick or stonework over many years, subsequent rainwater leaks tend to transmit brown stains through the wall. Even where a chimney has been out of action for decades this will continue to happen, making for some very unsightly marks where there has been dampness coming through to an internal wall.

The first thing to do is trace the leak which could be caused by cracked rendering on the stack, old flashings which have split or otherwise become faulty, degraded mortar which needs repointing, ineffective capping (out-of-service chimneys should be capped to allow air circulation but keep out the rain) or perhaps the capping or pot missing altogether through gale damage, smoke exit angled wrongly for prevailing weather system, etc. A more modern cause of leaks can be from a badly fitted TV aerial. A large aerial can impose a considerable burden on an old chimney stack in strong gale conditions and is sometimes better mounted elsewhere.

Having fixed the leak and allowed the dampness to dry out of the wall, any brown stains will need a special product to conceal them. Attempts with ordinary emulsion will appear satisfactory for a few hours, after which the stain will reappear. In some instances a good quality white undercoat will work, but if not, there are isolating paints available such as Isolfix, Rexfond, etc. These are more likely to be found in a specialist painting and decorating shop rather than a DIY superstore which tends to stock standard paints only. If all else fails, bring over a tin of Bitumen Isolating Primer on your next trip from the UK. This may be more readily available from a marine chandlers than elsewhere.

In some parts of the centre and north of the country the chimneys are very decorative and topped with ornate pots. It is not so easy to find suitable replacements these days so it is well worth making sure each chimney is thoroughly inspected and that whatever repointing or other necessary work is carried out when the roof is done. Often rather inaccessible due to their height, they are frequently ignored if they look sound.

Chimney stacks are shorter in the south where the roofs are not so steep, and they are therefore much easier to get at. One sometimes sees the imaginative use of pan tiles to form a little roof over the top, with holes on two or maybe all four sides for the smoke to exit. This is a good system which keeps all but really strongly driven rain out. The roof over the stack will normally be angled to match the main roof.

Cruder methods of reaching the same goal are often seen in the form of two or more bricks leant together to form a steeple over the hole and joined with mortar. The bricks used are normally the 25mm thick 40cm x 20cm honeycomb type in *terre cuite* (see diagram). This method (a) leaves a large opening for driven rain to enter. It is much more effective to lay the bricks horizontally (b) with overhangs (see diagram).

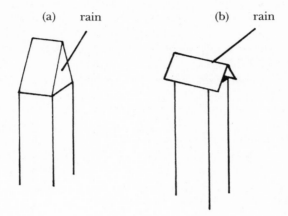

(a)   rain   (b)   rain

If the bricks can be angled to shelter the smoke exit against the weather so much the better. Although it is true that the south of the country is drier, when it does rain (especially in the autumn and early spring) it makes up for the lack at other times of the year and can be extremely heavy.

Material for flashings are available either in rigid zinc or by the roll in flexible aluminium/tar which can be cut as required. Properly installed, i.e. placed several inches under the tiles and cut in under any rendering, they will last for years, but the gulley formed where the upper side of the chimney stack meets the tiles should be occasionally checked for blockage. Leaves from any overhanging trees combined with soil and other materials carried by birds can lodge and eventually form a mound higher than the flashing and cause possible leaks where there are any slight faults.

Lucarnes

Known as dormer windows in the UK, these are in many different regional styles (like roofs) and the varying types make an interesting study while traversing France (see diagrams and photograph).

Repairs should be carried out like any other part of the main structure as regards tiles, stonework and gulleys. The internal wooden framework is normally a scaled down replica of the main roof timbers, but some have external timbers which decay over the years, replacement of which will call for a specialist carpenter (*charpentier*). Should the timber be sound, several coats of a good wood preservative are strongly recommended. (This also goes for any other external timberwork.)

In cases where a ruin is being restored and the *lucarne* has collapsed, or is otherwise damaged to the extent that the original design is unclear, a search will have to be made of other buildings locally to ascertain the style. Contact the library or the preservation society if there is one, or ask the *prefecture* to get in touch with the nearest A.N.A.H. (*Agence National pour Amelioration d'Habitat*) or the *Architect Conseil de Bâtiment de France*. All these organizations will give free advice, and the latter two may be able to supply plans which a local architect can turn into instruction for the builder.

Lucarnes

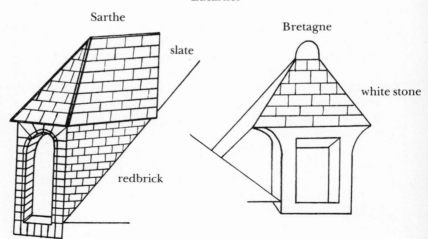

Starting from a ruin. The walls that were standing have been repointed and those that weren't, rebuilt. Notice the notches to accept new beams

The finished job, complete with swimming pool and small working vineyard. Some of the original shrubs and trees were carefully preserved

The beginnings of a roof terrace. The old plaster has been removed and the stonework is ready for repointing and rendering

Rendering for amateurs using the shuttering method, showing the sort of bracing necessary to hold the panels in place

The shuttering boards
removed, the walls are
now ready for stabilizing
with Resine d'Accrochage
and then painting

The drain hole is essential to any walled terrace. The original
shutters have been left in place so as not to spoil the façade

The top section of roof was retained to provide shelter. The vine will be trained around the three joists when big enough

An example of a *lucarne* on a detached house in Issoire (near Clermont Ferrand)

From a high vantage point numerous roof terraces are revealed
which would be unnoticeable from street level

Pan tiles contrasting with the more modern *'tuiles mechanique'*.
Notice the typical flashing used to seal roof to wall, and the two
chimney covers which are totally inadequate against driven rain

This typical southern old town roofscape shows the eleventh-
century cathedral at Agde with plane trees bordering the canal du
Midi in the background

A *remise* on the edge of a spacious market square in central
France ideally placed for conversion into a desirable dwelling

Normandy cottages which were originally single-storey now have
a *lucarne* added where the loft has become an extra room

A barn in the Dordogne which would make a good conversion
with plenty of living space

A Dordogne barn after a really well-planned conversion which
keeps most of the original character

Lucarnes

Ile de France

Bourgogne

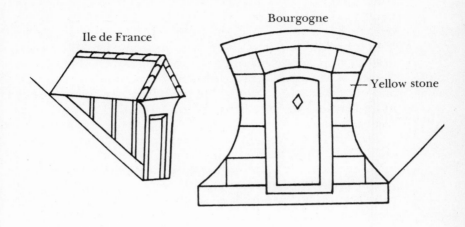

Yellow stone

Lucarnes

Presqui'ile du Cotentin

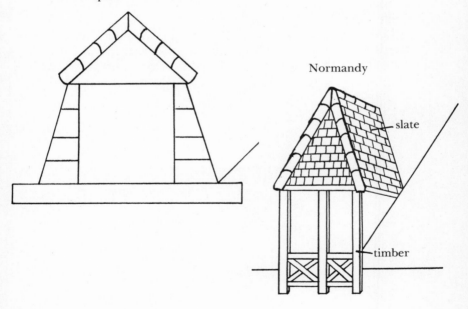

Normandy

slate

timber

Roof Terraces

Where a house has some land such as a courtyard, a patio or maybe a large balcony, there will be little need for such a terrace, but many town and village centre properties have no land beyond the four walls and many people like to eat or at least sit outdoors. This often involves taking chairs down to the street, an age old practice where neighbours get to chat and put the world to rights. On the whole, the British prefer more privacy, so for many, the roof terrace has proved an ideal solution.

The terrace is formed by removing part of the roof over one room, which then becomes a part of the exterior of the building and must be drained and weather-proofed as such.

The process is quite straightforward and even in strict conservation zones permission is usually granted as long as the actual façade is not affected. This will mean that the shutters are retained and also the lower rows of roof tiles. In other words, it is only when the shutters are open that anyone in the street looking up would know that anything has changed, because they would see the sky through the aperture rather than the original ceiling.

Building regulations usually limit the roof removal to one third of the whole roof area and should the terrace be higher than the normal floor level, i.e. when it is at loft level, there

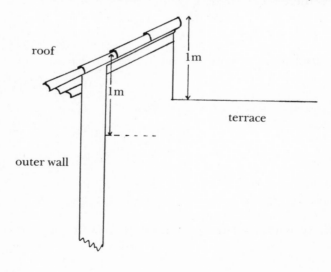

must be a metre depth at the lower (outside) edge as a safety precaution (see diagram). These regulations must be checked to make sure they apply to your particular region.

The main disadvantage of installing a roof terrace are the loss of all or part of a room and the fact that the adjacent rooms will get hotter in the summer and colder in the winter unless adequate measures are taken to insulate. This will mean not only double glazing the connecting door, but where the dividing wall is glazed, some sort of blinds or shutters will be needed to keep the heat of the sun out. These precautions may sound ridiculous if you are reading this in a UK winter, where sun and heat of any kind would be most welcome, but during the summer in the south of France the heat can become too much of a good thing.

Depending on the location of the house there might be little choice as to where the terrace can be sited. Sun worshippers usually opt for one as south facing as possible so that they can tan themselves all day. This is certainly the best position apart from the months of July and August, when the heat can be intense. One should bear in mind that the prevailing winds of this region – the Mistral and Tramontane – blow from the north and north west respectively, so the south facing terrace will exclude these completely and become a windless sun trap unless there is the possibility of an opening in that direction.

A south-east facing terrace will give some shade in the afternoon and evening and make a good compromise. As the summer sun gets up high at midday in the south, it is a good plan to leave some roof overhang both for shade and to provide a porch for weather protection over the door on to the terrace.

It doesn't have to be big to be of use. A space large enough for a picnic table and four chairs with a few extra inches to squeeze past is sufficient when internal space is short.

The main thing to remember is that the room, once protected by the roof, is now going to be subjected to the elements, so the floor must be made waterproof and adequately drained and the plaster which was good enough for an internal wall covering will have to be hacked off and rendered with sand and cement prior to being painted with a suitable exterior quality paint. It will not do to merely paint the plaster (no matter how waterproof the floor is made) as it will eventually get saturated and transmit dampness to the internal walls on the floor below.

The floor can be waterproofed in several ways. It is likely to be tiled in this country, so if the tiles are attractive enough to be re-used and are suitable for exterior use, they should first be lifted. In many old buildings it will be found that the layer of concrete under the tiles has decayed into loose powder which is probably best removed. Under this there are likely to be wooden boards, which are frequently to be found in excellent condition. If they are not, however, they need to be replaced as necessary and treated.

Provided the support under these boards has not been removed for some reason, it should be capable of supporting a concrete raft of similar thickness to the original and probably more. If in doubt seek expert advice. To take any spring out of the floor (fairly common in old buildings) the new concrete raft can be stiffened with iron mesh or rods which are obtainable from builders' suppliers such as MBM. Laying a polythene sheet membrane over the boards before floating on the concrete will save problems below.

If an area of heavy-duty glass tiles is to be incorporated into the terrace as a means of letting light down to the floor below this should be pre-planned, as should any wiring and pipe runs. (Water pipes to be buried in concrete should be run through PVC conduits large enough to allow for expansion. Wiring should be dealt with in the same way.)

The raft should be formed after the old plaster has been removed from the walls, so that the new rendering will come down over it at the edges.

The floor should be levelled carefully to discourage the formation of puddles. (It would be ideal, but seldom practical, to slope the floor towards the drain outlet. If it is possible, however, about 6mm per metre will do.) As concrete is difficult to level really well a self-levelling material known as *ragreage* can be used on the surface prior to tiling.

The hole through the wall which will form the drain should be carefully dealt with. Water should not be allowed to soak into the wall, so it should be lined with pan tiles inverted to form a gulley, well bedded in mortar and the sides of the aperture should be rendered. A slope of about 15cm is desirable in a wall about 60cm thick. If it has to be less, the part of the tile protruding outside should project at least 15.5cm or water will tend to run back underneath and down the wall, causing green stains at best and internal damp patches at worst. Alternatively it can be collected in a hopper and routed down through a drain pipe. (This might be necessary anyway if the drainage were to spill on to a neighbour's roof and cause ill-feeling.) The internal end should be set into the concrete raft and the floor tiles should overlap. As for forming the hole, old buildings tend to be built from stone of greatly varying sizes, especially those with thick walls in two layers and so finding conveniently placed stones to remove for the drain is not always easy. Sometimes it is advantageous to choose a different spot where the original excavation reveals a particularly massive stone.

Removing the roof should always be the last operation. That way the job will not be held up by bad weather, and rainwater will not be allowed in to cause problems before all is sealed.

Pan tiles, as previously described, merely rest on one another apart from the ridge and sometimes the gutter end, where they are fixed with mortar. Having removed part of the roof leaving tiles on top of the walls both to comply with regulations and to avoid any chance of the walls being saturated from above, the top row will need fixing with mortar, as they are now vulnerable to the wind. If it is desirable or expedient to leave any beams or joists in place, they should be well treated to withstand the weather.

Windows may be considered redundant, but if left in place will also need good weather-proofing treatment. Windows in France are made as an inward opening and therefore interior item. Although they might make a good wind-break it is normally sufficient just to have the shutters, which can be opened as required to admit a breeze or for admiring the view.

Another much less elaborate but equally effective way of achieving a watertight terrace, but is unlikely to find favour amongst traditional builders, is the use of GRP (glass reinforced plastic) as used in the boat and other industries.

This technique, which is for the floor only (the walls have to be treated as already described and rendered first in this case) can avoid having to remove the tiles, and being very lightweight will not impose any strain on the support below.

That GRP is eminently suitable for the job is proved by the fact that it is frequently used to line swimming pools, including those at roof-top level. It is imperative to use it properly though. It will not adhere to loose surfaces, or ones that are wet or greasy. It will stick to tiles up to a point, but they would have to be thoroughly degreased with acetone first. Perhaps the best procedure is to cover the floor area with 19mm chipboard (*aggloméré*), fill up any gaps with a mixture of resin and industrial talc (suitably catalysed) or use locally bought mastic polyester (the same type of product as Plastic Padding or Isopon in the UK).

GRP products are available at DIY superstores, at a price, and normally in small quantities, but they can be bought much more economically at the nearest GRP factory building boats, swimming pools, etc. You will probably have to provide your own containers, i.e. a ten litre plastic can for the resin (which should be bought pre-accelerated) and a small bottle for the catalyst (*catalyseur*). They will probably also sell acetone in bulk, so take something like a glass Perrier bottle.

With the accelerator already added, all that remains is to add around one per cent catalyst to the resin and this will give you between ten and twenty minutes working time. Consequently it is better to work with small quantities of around 0.5l. at a time (in an expendable jar or tin).

Soak a coat of resin into the chipboard and when this has dried apply another coat prior to laying the chopped strand mat (sheets of interwoven glass strands sold off a roll at the boatbuilders). The mat should be well saturated with resin (it goes translucent when saturated) either using a brush or roller. Both of these will have to be thrown away unless they are thoroughly cleaned with acetone soon after use.

For once, gravity is a friend, so take advantage and be generous with the resin to ensure a good seal. Those who favour belt and braces may apply a second layer of mat, but if the first was well laid it shouldn't be necessary. It is a good idea, however, to use up any spare resin by applying further coats, just to make sure there isn't even a pin hole uncovered.

The mat should also be applied three or four inches up the rendered walls, to form a tray. It is sometimes easier to do this as an addition using pre-cut sheets about eight inches wide. It should also extend into the pan tile drain a few inches. GRP sticks well to mortar provided the surface is cleaned of any loose particles beforehand. The process of laying the mat should be planned well so that the worker works his way to the door rather than getting stranded in the middle. It can be walked on about half an hour after application.

I have found that modern tile cements stick well to cured GRP, but some people like to sprinkle fine, washed sand on before it has dried as an aid to tile adhesion. It can't do any harm provided there is no sand left loose. Alternatively apply a coat of Resine D'Accrochage (see list of products at end of book).

The doorway leading from the terrace to an internal room should have a step or ledge to keep out rainwater. A wooden strip fastened under the door at least 10cm above the tiles will do. This can be screwed into the chipboard with silicone mastic used as a seal and the GRP should be formed into a lip as per around the walls. It is not necessary to use exterior grade chipboard because if the job is done thoroughly it will never get wet.

An alternative product to waterproof the floor with is Calandrite or a similar brand of aluminium/tar sheeting, as can be used in smaller sizes for flashings. This product comes in rolls of 10m x 1m. It is always applied with the aluminium surface uppermost, the area having been primed with a kind of liquid bitumen known as an 'impression', which is thick and glutinous and should fill up any cracks or holes effectively. The sheeting is then cut to suitable size, laid and the joins overlapped an inch or two and sealed by heating with a blowlamp and rolled flat. (The kind of roller used for wallpaper joints will do, but will need thorough cleaning well after use). The product can be laid on the original tiles, or sheets of ply or chipboard, but should be protected by exterior quality tiles. (Stiletto heels can puncture it.)

If using the above method, the Calandrite should be laid before the walls are rendered. It should, like the GRP, be turned a few inches up the stonework to form a tray, and then rendered down over to form a good seal. The use of this material is more likely to find favour with a builder, being a well used building material. If it is carefully applied it should be waterproof, but it is unlikely to form such a complete seal as GRP and with each roll costing upwards of £60, it will not be cheaper.

As a final aid to the comfort of sun worshippers, a shower head is often mounted on terraces. Either hot and cold or just a cold supply. The usual shower tray is unnecessary.

9   Floors

Much more use is made of floor tiles in France than in the UK. In old buildings these are likely to be in *terre cuite* faded to a dull red/brown or a highly patterned type not unlike marble. A lot are now in unobtainable sizes and long obsolete patterns, making replacement of broken tiles difficult if not impossible. This is often a matter of compromise; *terre cuite* can sometimes be bought in larger sizes and cut down and assiduous searching will sometimes be rewarded by finding the marble type in a compatible colour and design.

Occasionally tiles crack for apparently no good reason apart from old age, but more often and especially where quite a few are broken it can be taken as an indication of problems underneath.

The traditional construction method was rough floor boarding laid over joists supported by beams, or sometimes laid over smaller beams which were closer together. A layer of concrete was then spread over the boards up to about 5 cm thick, and then the tiles were laid.

Where the concrete has decayed over a long period, and softened, thus becoming inefficient at supporting the tiles, they can crack when walked on.

Alternatively the problem can be in the timber – rotten boarding, joists or, in extreme cases, the beams themselves. On the other hand, the timber might be sound, but capable of movement where the support into the wall has loosened or softened. As already discussed, this can happen during the process of renovation when rendering and plaster is hacked off a wall beneath and found to be all that was supporting the joists or beams. It can even be caused by previous alterations where a supporting wall has been removed.

Problem floors are often ones that were originally lofts that

Tiling over Floor Boards

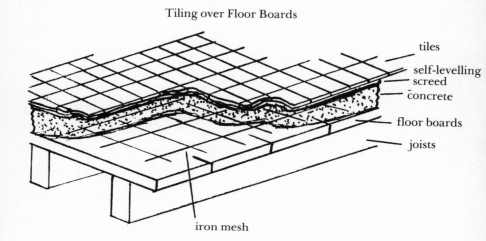

tiles
self-levelling screed
concrete
floor boards
joists
iron mesh

were never as strongly supported as the floors below, being intended for light storage only. In these days when every cubic metre counts and every floor (*plancher*) is used for living accommodation, sometimes extra strengthening is needed, in the form of additional beams or joists, where it was previously unnecessary.

To take the most extreme case first. Where the supporting beams and joists are too far gone to safely carry out their function, the whole floor will have to be demolished and replaced. The question is how? By modern methods or traditionally? A common building procedure is to install a brick and lintel floor. This is simply a matter of laying lintels (steel reinforced concrete joists) wall to wall and embedded in the wall at each end, as would be a wooden joist or beam, spaced so as to accept a type of brick (normally 40cm) specially moulded for the purpose, which slots in between each lintel. Once laid, the top surface, i.e. the floor, is levelled with a concrete raft prior to tiling and the underside is plastered and becomes the ceiling of the room below.

This is a very efficient, strong and relatively inexpensive way of replacing a floor. It should also be waterproof and so is ideal where a roof terrace is planned above. The lintels are not as massive to move as a large wooden beam and can usually be muscled into place by a couple of fit builders. Perhaps the only disadvantage is one of authenticity; the ceiling below now lacks beams and thus may not have the visual appeal you would like. This, of course, is largely a matter of personal choice, as would be, dare I mention it, the installation of some false beams made from GRP and polyurethane foam. These are readily available from building superstores and are amazingly realistic, with the added bonus of being very light in weight, so fairly easy to transport and install.

For many, though, there is just nothing like the real thing. New beams can be bought from timber suppliers, at a price (expect to pay upwards of 350 francs (approximately £35) per metre length for a 30cm square beam – 1991 price). Those wishing for something even more authentic than this will find second-hand beams at some demolition depots which will be a little, though often not much cheaper, but will look better when installed, having already aged. As demolition contractors will have heavy equipment for moving large objects, it might be possible to strike a deal on delivery and installation at the time of purchase.

It is likely that even second-hand beams and joists will cost more than a new brick and lintel floor, and there may also be the problem of access for large beams if the house is up a narrow alley in a town or village centre.

Whether new or second-hand, the timber should always be well treated with a good brand of rot inhibitor and worm killer while all the surfaces are easy to get at.

Perhaps the most common case is where the main beams are sound, or at least sufficiently so, with suitable treatment, to do their job for another century or so, but some of the joists are cracked, distorted or decayed (often only where embedded in the wall). Or maybe just the surface boarding has suffered the ravages of time. Both of the latter are relatively simple to replace, but it should be borne in mind that if the floor is to be once more rafted with concrete and tiled again, this is no time for false economy or for the hiding of potential problems. Getting at them again will be a major operation. If in doubt, rip it out, is a good motto here. Any timber in a dubious state, especially if it is suffering from dry or wet rot should be removed to stop it spreading. Worm damage is often limited to the surface and can be killed off, but be generous with the use of treatments and call in expert help if unsure.

The boarding can be replaced by tongued and grooved timber or tongued and grooved chipboard, but before this is done, any new wire or piping runs should be installed.

With floors where there is movement, for whatever reason, it is not possible to just level off any depressions and retile. Before too long the new tiles will start breaking up. It is inadvisable (but often done) to float on another concrete raft. This will cover up the underfloor troubles for a few years, and if the raft is steel reinforced it will last for longer. There are disadvantages, however. First of all if the problem was one of dry or wet rot in the timber, the decay will continue until eventually something will have to be done – only now it will be a lot more difficult and time (and money) consuming. Secondly, by raising the floor level by the height of the new raft and tiles, there will have to be a step up somewhere, which can be a nuisance, if not dangerous. Thirdly the extra weight might be too much for the support below.

All in all, it usually makes good sense to lift the tiles and the old concrete, renew what is necessary and end up with the floor at its original level.

Tiles are a very practical floor covering and easy to keep clean. They do, however, have one snag: that of noise, suffered by those on the floor below. In an apartment, this can cause friction with the downstairs neighbours, especially when those above wear hard tipped shoes. Plenty of rugs can be a solution, or even paying (or sharing the payment) for insulation to be installed on the ceiling below. Alternatively a false floor can be built, where there is good headroom.

As with any additional floor, there will be the problem of a step, so if there is plenty of headroom, make it a good one. A proper step of between 15cm and 20cm is less likely to trip people up than a small one that is easily unnoticed.

The method is to lay wooden joists on the original floor, usually at about 40cm centres, fill up in between them with insulation, such as rock wool, for sound deadening, then board them over. Tongued and grooved pin boards can look very good just varnished. (In France these are tongued and grooved on the ends as well as the sides, so there is no need to join each one over a joist.) Alternatively the joists can be covered with chipboard flooring which is then suitable for tiling, laying decorative parquet, carpet, etc.

Where the original floor is found to be sound, but the old tiles dirty or dulled, these can be treated as follows. The dirt of ages, even cement, can be removed by scrubbing with a solution of *chlorhydrique* (hydrochloric) acid – one measure of acid to four of water. (Wear suitable protection such as goggles, rubber gloves and overalls. Have very good ventilation and wear a face mask.) Having dried, glazed tiles can be polished with one of many brands of tile cleaner found in the local supermarket, and *terre cuite* (unglazed) tiles can be treated with a 50/50 mixture of white spirit and linseed oil (*huile de lin*) applying as many coats as necessary until the tiles stop absorbing.

10 Ceilings

The actual construction of the ceiling (*plafond*) in the average old French house will, of course, be the same as the floors as discussed in the last chapter (apart from when the upper level is opened up to expose the under side of the roof) as the ceiling will be the underside of all floors except the ground.

With the exception of the *grenier*, there is usually no lack of headroom in old French houses and so one frequently finds false ceilings of lathe and plaster attached to a line of joists a foot or so under the beams – presumably to decrease the cubic area of the room to make it easier to heat. This sometimes leaves a large gap between the ceiling and the floor above which is handy for the plumber and electrician to install new wiring and pipe runs, but otherwise, with more efficient forms of heating, could be called wasted space.

These false ceilings, and others built in the same fashion, but attached to the underside of the beams, are often very decorative with moulded edgings and roses, some of which can be replaced with modern plastic replicas. To demolish or leave will obviously be very much a matter of personal taste; a preference for the elegant or rustic, because removing this ceiling will expose the beams above. Sometimes the ceiling will be in a very bad state and make this decision easier.

Presuming that the state of the ceiling makes demolition the obvious choice, it should be done as early in the overall renovation programme as possible, as with hacking off old plaster and rendering from the walls, it is a very messy job which will produce a lot of dust.

The usual procedure is to clear away all the lathe and plaster from the joists or beams, and replace it with plaster board, taping up the joins with brown paper tape, pre-soaked in water and skimmed with an *enduit* (filler) specially made for the job. (The same *enduit* also sticks the paper tape in place.) Subsequently, ceiling roses and covings etc. can be added if required.

Those who like a very rustic finish might like to leave out the last operation, especially where there was no false ceiling, because removal of the lathe and plaster will expose not only the beams, but the underside of the floorboards, although both may need work and wood treatment to make them look attractive. The disadvantages will be noise from people walking above, difficulty in concealing wiring or pipes and a very dark ceiling which will make the room somewhat sombre.

A good compromise is to line in between the beams with plasterboard or when more insulation or sound deadening is desirable, plasterboard backed with polystyrene, or rockwool packed above the plasterboard. Tongued and grooved white pine with a clear varnish will also create a very warm effect and contrast well with the darker wood of the beams.

On the top floor, where the false ceilings have been removed to create more space and expose the underside of the roof, it may be possible to expose the joists as well as the beams. Wedging the insulation and plasterboard between them. In a lot of cases though, these will have been doubled up alongside old joists which are cracked or split, making it probably better to cover them and just leave the beams exposed.

Where a building has an actual top floor rather than just a loft (especially in the southern part of the country where the roofs are not so steep as in the north) the removal of false ceilings can make a really dramatic difference. Often the dividing walls can be removed as well (or some of them) turning two or three cramped little rooms in to a spacious living area. With perhaps a part opened up to form a roof terrace, the top floor now has the best of all worlds.

Putting up plasterboard ceilings is definitely one of the more tiresome building tasks. Gravity is the enemy again and the boards are not only heavy, but also delicate and easily damaged. It is also desirable to keep the panels as large as possible to minimize the number of joins. Some of the superstores now hire out platforms on which the board is laid and then jacked up to ceiling level. This can be a great help where a couple of helpers cannot be found.

Needless to say, with the irregularities of old buildings the panel will seldom fit first time, however careful the measuring, so it will have to be offered up and then lowered again for reshaping, sometimes not for the last time. Putting up tongued and grooved pine strips (*lambris*) is a lot easier on the muscles.

A visit to any of the large superstores (Mr Bricolage, Castorama, OBI, etc.) will show that a complete range of paints, panels, wallpapers, false beams, decorative polystyrene and cork tiles and numerous mouldings is available in good quality and prices not that dissimilar to the UK.

11 Some Practical Features and Innovations

Letting in Light

In the northern part of France and parts of the centre and west there tends to be more detached old property outside the confines of town and village. Most of these have some land or a garden, so light can be let in on two or more sides. The problem of dinginess applies more to the town and village centre houses all over France, especially in the south, where efforts were made to actually keep the light out.

To some extent this was done with good reason, as during the high summer admitting light meant admitting heat as well, and this can be quite extreme at times. On the other hand, the price of keeping out the heat was to render the place gloomy and even cold for the other nine or ten months of the year. Nowadays, with the benefits of double glazing, efficient insulation and the use of modern materials for the construction of such things as vertical, swivelling blinds, there is much more control over the elements, allowing for larger windows without discomfort.

There are various ways of brightening the gloomiest house, however restricted its position. Perhaps the most obvious is to enlarge the windows, but in some historic zones this may be forbidden by planning regulations. In this case it helps to angle the reveals so that the aperture on the inner wall is wider than that on the outside (see diagram).

The use of white paint on the reveals and generally inside the room will make a big difference, as will mirrors placed to reflect light to other parts of the room. Lovers of rustic decor who favour interior walls of bare stone or brick combined with dark ceilings of exposed beams and boards often have to

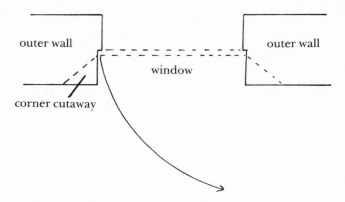

pay the price by keeping lights on all day.

If you have a terraced apartment with the usual one window per room, the above ideas may be the best you can do, but those on the top floor, or who own the whole building can gain enormous benefit from the roof.

Roof terraces have already been mentioned. An additional advantage of these is that one or more walls will connect with the interior room rather than the façade and as such may have windows let into them without affecting planning controls. In fact, a lot of designers of terraces have one or more entire walls in glass, either fixed or opening, letting enormous amounts of light through. If this is south facing though, some thought will have to be given to keeping out the summer heat.

Those in the north or who otherwise don't want to go to the extent of building a roof terrace can gain a lot of light by removing the upper ceilings to expose the roof and installing a skylight. Alternatively they could replace an area of roof tiles with glass ones, which are still available for most types of tile, and remove the lining immediately underneath. (The upper ceilings provide a certain amount of insulation against heat and cold, so their removal will mean insulating the underside of the roof.)

This will brighten up the top floor and for those who like living at the top and sleeping on the lower floors this might suffice, but if not, the glass tiles, roof window or skylight should be placed above the back wall of the house (in the case of back-to-back terraced homes) and then if about a metre of each floor is removed, right down to the ground floor if necessary, a well will be created letting in light all the way down. The type of building where this is necessary is not likely to be large. We are probably talking about widths and lengths of six metres or less, so it will not be a major job.

Where the beams run toward the back wall, they can be left in place and merely the last two or three joists removed, plus the boards and tiles (if any). Where they run across and there is no handy beam a metre or so in from the wall, the joists will have to be sawn off at the required length and maybe supported by an additional joist or beam. All that remains to do now is to trim the open end of the floor with a board (where joist ends are to be hidden) and erect a balustrade for security. To make the job simpler, the joists don't even have to be removed, as plenty of light will still be allowed down past them.

Stairwells and staircases can often be good transmitters of light if removed and replaced by the open spiral or straight step type, but obviously this would only be done where the gain in light would be significant or where both were in a bad state of repair.

Where the front door is of no particular significance or in bad repair, replacement with a glazed or semi-glazed door can allow in as much light as a window and do much to brighten up the hallway or entry room. In some zones though, this might contravene regulations, in which case it might be possible to open up a small window above it. Some old buildings already have one, the most frequent type being the traditional *oeil-de-boeuf* (bull's eye). These are still available at the large woodwork superstores such as Lapeyre and are either the opening or fixed type which both come with a frame. There will also be a choice of triangular or rectangular windows for the same purpose.

Where a glazed door is considered to be a security weak point, the same company also market plain or ornate steel grills to cover the glazed area.

Balconies
Unlike roof terraces, balconies, being an external appendage are usually very limited in size, and few are large enough to

accommodate a table and chairs for devotees of alfresco eating. Unless massively supported from underneath, there are structural reasons to restrict the size to about 75cm. (There might also be planning restrictions as well.) In some cases it is possible to solve this problem by having it all or partly internal.

Most balconies are served by an access door or at least a full length window. Where this is not as wide as the balcony and planning permission is forthcoming, it can be opened up or doubled until it is part of the interior given up to form an extension. Sometimes, where the walls are very thick, this need only be the depth of the wall itself to gain sufficient area, but if more space is required then an internal wall will have to be built, complete with access door, to keep the weather out and where the original balcony entrance is to be removed and left open, the floor area up to the new internal wall will need to be watertight as for a roof terrace. As the roof or ceiling is not touched, you are not limited to any particular floor.

Mezzanine Floors
Where there is sufficient height, a mezzanine floor is a very practical way to gain more floor area within the confines of the original walls. A height of not less than five metres is needed to give enough headroom above and below. A bit like an internal balcony, it is normally only a part floor or gallery at one end or side of the room, served by its own staircase and balustraded for security.

Not all rooms will have this sort of headroom, but some have, especially where ceilings are being removed to expose the underside of the roof. It is also often feasible in a barn or remise. Where a mezzanine is constructed below the roof, it is not necessary to have full standing headroom throughout. The most important thing is to have it at the top of the staircase, if it then slopes down with the angle of the roof it is not that inconvenient. A height of as little as 1.5m (just under 5ft) or even less is not a problem where it would be, for instance, on the side of the bed you don't get out of, for children's bed space, sitting space or storage.

The French tend to treat all their woodwork with dark stains, which can make the area below the mezzanine a bit oppressive. With both balustrade and floor boards in white pine and clear varnish this makes the ceiling underneath a pleasant feature. Balustrading and stairs can both be bought from the woodwork superstores, but they can also be easily made by an enthusiastic carpenter (see diagram).

Simple Balustrade Using 15mm Dowels

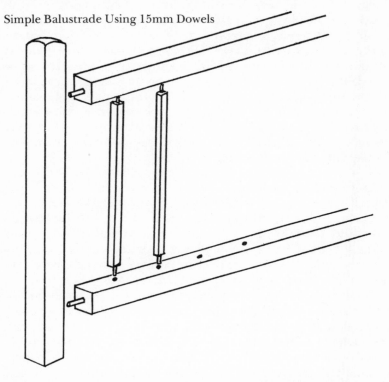

Where space is short the steps up to the mezzanine can be a little steeper than usual and can rise up two metres or so taking up an area of only 1.5m x 60cm. A small spiral staircase needs only a square area of 1.25m to rise in. Being open, neither the straight or spiral staircase block light.

Wood or Coal Burning Fires and Fireplaces
Very popular all over France as a means of heating and in some cases cooking as well, an open or a decorative closed fire can make a very attractive feature in any room. Obviously the coal or wood burning type will need a chimney, either in brick or with a hood venting into a steel

conduit. Imitation coal or wood fires worked by gas need an exhaust, which can just go through an external wall where there is no convenient chimney.

Electric fires need no venting and a glass-doored stove with a red bulb inside can look so realistic when alight that one can be fooled into extending hands towards it for warming.

Very attractive, old and ornate stoves can be found in antique shops (which will either be called *Brocante* or *Antiquities* in working order. Alternatively, modern, ultra efficient but less attractive replicas can be bought in the large stores or specialist shops. Complete with conduits, joints, waterproof smoke stacks, etc. There are also many manufacturers of brick and stone fireplaces, often sold in kit form for home completion. Many are complete with log space and cooking griddles.

Exposing Plastered Beams

It will be noticed in many old buildings that the beams are plastered and painted to blend in with the ceiling. Some will prefer to leave them that way, but devotees of the rustic usually like to expose wood wherever possible. It is as well to know, perhaps before the decision is made, that these beams will involve more work to achieve a nice finish.

Plaster doesn't stick very well to smooth wood, so when it is removed it will be seen that the beam has been roughened by regular chipping with an adze (an old tool like an axe, but with the blade at right angles to the handle) to provide a more suitable surface.

This will provide the enthusiast with quite a few hours work to chisel off all the raised chips to end up with a nicer but much dented surface that will look good when treated or varnished.

Archways

Many old buildings once had archways where there are now dividing walls. Often these are of the Gothic pointed arch style. The bonus of uncovering such treasures is one of the few compensations for the rigorous task of hacking off the old plaster and rendering in the course of renovating the walls. Very old town and village property will have often been subdivided over the years, so it is not all that unusual for an arch to be exposed on a party wall. Obviously in this case it cannot be opened up, and anyway it might not be desirable to do so. It still looks very impressive, however, if just the stonework of the arch is left exposed and the rest of the wall plastered. A connecting door will often be found in the centre of a bricked up archway.

Lintels and Corner-stones

Exposed stonework, by virtue of its antiquity seems to promote a sense of timelessness to some rooms. Where there is too much will, however, this may result in making the room dark and gloomy. Just by picking out the lintels above windows and doors and in some cases the corner-stones of the window reveals (where they are of good, distinct shape) can put several attractive features into a room otherwise plastered. Additionally, some large beams rest on equally large stones which often project into the room. Plastering these over merely creates a bulge in the wall, whereas bared and cleaned they can look very impressive. All this can apply to the exterior of the building as well, where corner-stones and lintels can be picked out to advantage on an otherwise rendered wall surface. Getting all the old plaster out of the stone, especially volcanic basalt which is pock marked with holes, is time consuming but worth it. A wire brush and a pointed tool of some sort will be necessary.

Nooks and Alcoves

On very thick old stone walls, it is usually possible to create an alcove by removing part of the inner half, providing a suitable lintel can be found, either arched or straight. The back surface can then be repointed and/or rendered and plastered if desired, or just left as bare stone. As well as gaining space, this can also have the effect of giving an otherwise featureless room an attractive focal point.

On a much smaller scale, during the repointing process there may be revealed a stone which forms a natural lintel over three smaller stones beneath it. In this case there is no reason why the centre stone should not be removed and an old *terre cuite* tile set into the base to form a nook suitable for an ornament, small flower pot, etc.

Features are an intensely personal thing and the ways of

making the décor more interesting and practical are endless. Some ideas are better than others, some created by the imaginative mind of an artist and others just to perform a useful purpose. Few can be as innovative as one I saw, designed to bring warmth and interest to an otherwise dull and cramped little room. One wall, a party wall as it happened, had a glazed and fixed door mounted over an alcove, behind which was a vividly realistic scene depicting a swimming pool backed by a beautiful pine fringed beach and the blue sea beyond, with a bright blue sky above. Directly through the door was a diving board and the whole thing, especially when lit up with concealed lighting, was so well done and with such appeal one felt a distinctive urge to open the door, walk out on the springboard and dive in. Though completely false it all had a very real practical value in giving the illusion of space and warmth.

In some cases a feature can be used to hide something. There are things such as electric fuse boards and gas meters that are better concealed by a cupboard or even just a curtain.

Those in search of ways to improve the general ambience and décor will find lots of good ideas in the local library and the French equivalents of magazines of the *Homes and Gardens* type. A good selection of these glossy productions will be found in the local paper shop, which will often be called *maison de la presse*.

12 Windows and Shutters

With very rare exceptions, windows (*fenêtres*) in France open inwards and shutters (*volets*) open outwards.

To deal with windows first – this system has the advantage that the woodwork is better protected from the elements and so should last longer. On the other hand, when buying replacements (which are still available in most styles), it is as well to bear in mind that because the window is considered an interior-quality item, some will be offered at a lower price, but made from inferior-quality wood. There will often be a choice between Oak (*chêne*, usually described as *chêne massif* which denotes that it is solid oak rather than oak veneer), *bois exotique*, which applies to red woods like mahogany or *sapin du nord*, which is northern pine, and a soft wood, which will be less durable than the first two hard wood types.

Windows bought from any large *menuiserie* (bulk woodwork supplies) will almost never be glazed, but the glass can be supplied separately, cut to size and in various qualities – both in double and single glazing. Putty, fixing nails, handles, locks, etc. are also supplied separately, the industry being very much angled towards home completion. Generally speaking, the quality and construction of all joinery items bought in France is excellent, but, as with all wooden structures, needs regular treatment or painting to keep it so.

The main disadvantage of inward opening windows is the difficulty of finding a restrainer that will hold the window partially open and still look nice. There are gadgets on the market to adjust the aperture, but few that will enhance the look of the internal wall, hence in most cases the window must be fully open, shut, or left prey to being slammed by a sudden draught. Where the window is placed so that there is an area of internal sill, anything placed on it must be removed before opening the window. Finally, the joint between the frame and the window aperture must be one hundred per cent watertight, especially along the bottom, or rain could cause internal dampness and decay the plaster. Of course, the latter problem can be solved by closing the shutters, but who wants to do that in the middle of the day?

Because of its more protected position, a French-made window tends to be of more sophisticated design than its UK counterpart, most being virtually airtight and certainly completely draught-proof when closed. This even applies to double windows, which have a groove on one side and a tongue on the other and thus have to be closed simultaneously. Some older models are beautifully engineered with one concave and one excave edge to marry up tightly when closed. They are designed for efficiency as well as elegance. No passage of air, however, means no ventilation and this situation can leave a draught-conditioned Brit feeling somewhat stifled. Few windows in France have those convenient, small, opening sections at the top. Its all or nothing here.

During the night, ventilation can be improved by opening a window and letting air in through the close shutters, which are seldom draught-proof. This way you can also dictate at what hour you want the daylight coming into the room, as shutters are more effective at keeping out light than curtains.

When buying old property it will be almost certain that the windows will need at least some attention, even if it is only a question of stripping and repainting and a new pane or two of glass, but it is just as likely that repairs will be needed or even replacement.

If the work necessary entails removing the window and setting it up on a bench, it will depend on its age whether this operation is extremely simple or very difficult. Most relatively modern hinges separate one half from the other merely by opening the window to ninety degrees and lifting it off. Before that hinges had pins that could be easily extracted, maybe after the application of a little oil and some gentle encouragement applied by hammer and punch to the bottom of the pin. It is when the pin refuses to move that the problems begin. These sort of old iron hinges are liable to fracture if treated too violently. Time and humidity are a very effective combination for rusting things up solidly. So, if the window had been closed up and unused for years, even the act of forcing it open can damage the hinges beyond repair and it won't do the woodwork any good either.

Patience and penetrating oil and/or the very prudent use of heat from a blowlamp will usually eventually bear fruit. With the window open, but the hinge pin irremovable it may be necessary to remove the whole hinge, an operation which can bring tears of angry frustration to the uninitiated.

It must be remembered that it was the French who, a century or two ago, invented the mystery clock; so called because only an extremely shrewd expert could tell how it worked, lacking, as it did, key, spring or pendulum. A similar brain must have designed this type of hinge.

In their continual quest for elegance and style, French designers obviously worked on the principle that if something couldn't look good then it shouldn't be seen at all. So it is with the mystery hinge. The first thing that becomes evident is the invisibility of any part of the hinge beyond the pin and the sleeves around it. There is no sign of screws or other fastenings. A bit like an iceberg, three quarters of it are lurking beneath the surface. In fact, the flats of the hinge are slotted into the wood of the frame and window at an angle of approximately forty-five degrees. When this is discovered, the apparent absence of any other fastening can make it appear that the hinge was originally driven into its slot as a tight fit and can now be extracted accordingly. One could certainly be forgiven for attempting this, especially as by this stage your temper is liable to be wearing a little thin, but considerable damage will result from using brute force. This is because nails were driven through the woodwork, passing through holes in the flats to keep the hinges firmly in place, but subsequent layers of paint will have completely hidden them. The number of nails depends on the size of the hinges, but there are usually not more than three. A careful scraping away of the paint in the hinge region will reveal them and chiselling out a little wood to get a grip on the heads will be necessary.

Replacement of a broken hinge of this type is still sometimes possible in a traditional village ironmongers. Sadly though, many of these fascinating old shops are being replaced by modern DIY stores whose first operation seems to entail clearing out all the old (useful) stock. The other alternative, as for so many things, is to scour the local tip. Most builders involved with modernizing old property simply dump all the old doors and windows. The labour-intensive business of woodwork repair is not so cost effective as rapid replacement with new items. Thus apart from the possibility of finding good hinges on broken old windows, it is not unknown to find windows and shutters in better conditions than yours, and in the right sizes. If you should happen to come across such treasures and have transport available, seize them at once, even if you haven't reached the stage of repairing the windows yet. For one thing, you may not be alone in your search and in any case the local authorities think nothing of destroying these useful items by fire or bulldozing.

Failure to find a replacement mystery hinge will mean going over to the modern type, but now the screws will show and the flats will need to be made flush with the woodwork. The shots of the old hinges are best filled with a sliver of wood and glued in.

When buying the modern hinge, often to be found loose in the bins of a DIY store, it is important to select left- or right-hand hinges as required. This is not as obvious as it sounds because they all look the same when assembled and they are often taped up in pairs denying the possibility of close scrutiny. The convenience of being able to lift the window (or door) of the frame, once opened to ninety degrees to clear, means that the half fastened to the frame must have the pin – the male in other words – and the half on the door – the female part – must be hollow. They are also available in pairs, but these will be one left- and one right-hand hinge, two or three pairs of which are intended for double windows. Hang on to the till receipt in case they need changing.

With the window removed it will now be easy to inspect and work on. Most old windows have multiple, small panes of glass. If these must be removed the job should be done with care as they will probably be 2mm glass and very brittle. It is seldom possible to buy 2mm glass now as the thinnest normally used these days is 3mm, and as the woodwork tends to be very slender, there is not much depth for the fixing nails and putty, so every millimetre counts. New panes also look more perfect and so stand out noticeably. As with hinges, old glass will often be found on the tip in sizes large enough to cut down.

The frame will normally be held in place by two or more flat brackets on each side, which, if properly fitted, will be let in to the wood and plaster and thus not easy to find once painted. This isn't always so, though, in which case their whereabouts will be obvious. Removal will cause at least some damage to the plaster, but this can be minimized by cutting immediately round each bracket with a sharp brick chisel so as to be left with just a minor filling job.

Window locking mechanisms were originally blacksmith made and very robust, so they are often found to be still in good condition. In any case, these fittings, (known as *espagnolettes*) are still available. It is more usual to find the top and bottom studs which the fastener locks around broken or missing. Where these were set in wood, a screw bolt of slightly greater diameter than the original should be wound in and then the head cut off. If set in stonework it will be a case of finding a piece of rod or maybe a bolt which is a tight fit in the hole, and driving it in with a heavy hammer. You should first measure the depth with something thinner to make sure sufficient stonework will be left exposed for the fastener to lock around.

Where the stone has broken out around the hole, the lower one can be set in with rapid drying cement (*ciment prompt*), but in the case of the top one gravity is working against you. Boring the hole deeper with a suitable masonry drill and driving in a longer stud is sometimes easier.

When it comes to repainting, it will be noticed that the French normally don't use a primer, just an undercoat (*sous couche*) and top coat. For traditionalists who feel a primer is necessary, one normally used on steelwork called Minium has the consistency of red lead and can be bought in grey or bright orange.

Always order new panes of glass which are a loose fit (especially in the south of France) with at least 2mm clearance on each side. This is even more important during the winter, because expansion in the heat of summer can cause tight panes to crack.

When replacing the windows it is seldom possible to find an exact fit. Most frames can, however, be pared down a little without removing too much strength, which is easier than cutting out the stone. It is often necessary though to buy a smaller size and set it into a subsidiary frame.

Arched single and double windows are available, at a price, and can sometimes be found in suitable sizes, but if not it will be necessary to have window and frame specially made by a joiner (*ébéniste*). One way to economize here is to fit a rectangular window into the vertical part of the aperture and install fixed glazing into the arch, separated by a wooden cross member. A glass cutting factory will be found on the industrial estates of most large towns and their prices are usually considerably less than a local shop, some of whom will use the same factory and add on their own commission.

Shutters
Very few French homes are without shutters which are usually on every window. New homes are no exception, even though the advent of double glazing makes them less vital than before, when they provided additional protection against the heat and cold. A building without shutters, in France, would look conspicuously incomplete.

Apart from serving as a first defence against the elements, they are also a good security device, as they lock from the inside. While this might not stop a determined burglar, he at least has twice the work of his UK counterpart in the course of gaining entry. Where they are a good fit and in sound condition, he might even look around for somewhere easier to break in to.

Shutters are of much simpler construction than windows and correspondingly easier to repair or replace. Even when they are missing altogether, having rotted away over the years through neglect, it should be clear from the hinge pins where the replacements are to go.

In very old buildings with thick walls and small windows, they will often be placed within the aperture so that when open they do not extend beyond the outside of the wall. In this position they will rest parallel to each other and can be held open by a wooden bar which drops in to slots on the inside surface of each shutter.

On more modern buildings they will either be fitted externally, or, preferably for their own weather protection, in to a
shallow recess which frames the window aperture, thus when
closed the top edge gets some shelter. In both the latter cases
the shutters will swing through 180 degrees and fasten against
the outer wall of the house held in place by a turnbuckle fixed
to the wall about half way along the bottom edge of the
shutter, known as an *arrêt de façade*.

Both this and the hinge pins (*gonds*) originally just had
spiked shafts for driving into the stonework. Nowadays they
can be supplied to fix in five different ways: a split shaft for
bedding in with *ciment prompt*, a flat shaft for fixing to the
wall with screws, a screw-threaded shaft for using in combination with a plug (*cheville*), a shaft in the form of an expanding
bolt and finally a decorative iron plate for surface fixing.

As in the case of windows, *espagnolette* fastenings are still
available, although the standard lengths of today may need
modification to fit the aperture in an old building. This is just a
matter of buying an *espagnolette* longer than the height of the
aperture, separating it into two parts by undoing the two nuts
where the handle is clamped on. It will now be found that the
rod is in two pieces, held together by the handle clamp. The
longer piece should now be cut down by the required amount,
making the whole fastening some 20mm shorter than the
window aperture, and clamped back together, making sure
that the top and bottom hooks are in the right position to do
their job of hooking around the studs when the handle is in the
closed position.

If you are lucky enough to find an old *espagnolette*, which
will often have a much more decorative handle, shortening or
extending it will be a welding job for the local blacksmith or
steel fabricator who will either cut the ends off, shorten as
necessary and reweld the ends back on, or ditto but add to the
length.

Replacement shutters can be made up from 25mm flooring
timber which is conveniently tongued and grooved, and they
will keep their shape for longer if the edge is glued, or planks
butt joined with a wooden dowel every 40cm or 50cm to stop
any tendency to sag once vertical. A 'z' frame on the inside
surface provides extra strength apart from the top and bottom
member serving as backing timber for the strap hinges.

Most old shutters are made from pine of one sort or another, now sold as *sapin* or *sapin du nord*. When carrying out repairs it is always best to get as near as possible to the original material as each has its own rate of expansion, contraction and water absorption. Like types make a less conspicuous repair and glue together better.

Doors

It will be noticed when buying doors in France that they come complete with frame (*bloc porte*). It is possible to buy the two elements separately, as it is is to buy the door on its own, but more normal to buy it complete.

By complete, this will include hinges, door locks (basic type, more sophisticated ones can be added later) etc. If the door is to be glazed, the glass, putty and fixing nails will be supplied, but not normally fitted.

In most cases the frame will have a five centimetre rebate ready for mating to five centimetre interior type wall bricks or plaster blocks.

Expendable battens will be stapled in position to hold the door and frame rigid. If it can be fixed in place like this it will ensure that the door is perfectly regular in its aperture and the locks work. Once the battens are removed the whole lot is liable to distortion and even a slight discrepancy can stop the lock bolt from fitting nicely into the striker plate.

Sometimes, of course, when the door is the only access to a room it will have to be removed from the frame, but it is advisable to first have the wall fitted to one side of it and at least the first two bricks fitted to the other (so one can step over) before removing the battens. This way it should be vertical (if the wall is) and a good fit. Holes should be made in the floor to accommodate the bottom of the frame and hold it rigid, and these should be regulated for depth so as to give a gap of 5mm or so at the bottom of the door. Beware discrepancies in the floor though, which might cause the door to stick on opening. (A long spirit level will reveal whether this might be the case).

When the wall is plastered, the plaster comes flush with the outer edge of the frame, and the joint is usually covered with half round beading, rather than architrave as normal in the UK.

13   Plumbing

Although entirely coincidental, the chapter number is perhaps fitting for this particular subject, which has been known to cause its fair share of grief.

There are many good, trained plumbers in France, but there also seems to be an equal number of very dubious operators. Many of these got started by doing their own plumbing (*plomberie*), then a neighbour's, the word spreading until the money was better than the regular job. This sequence of events isn't always a bad thing, in cases where someone gets involved in a trade because they enjoy it, they often work to a very high standard. Unfortunately, many are in it purely for the money and not averse to taking short cuts in pursuit of a quick profit.

It is usually these short cuts that cause future problems to occur; during the next winter freeze-up, for example, where staircases turn into waterfalls and eventually glaciers. There are many other horror stories which, even when settled by the insurance company, are a very nasty shock for the returning occupant, and are also likely to have a sting in the tail when the next water bill comes. ‘

Of course, freak winters are rare, but beware, even in the supposedly sunny south it can happen. A good example was January 1985, when night temperatures were recorded as low as $-26°C$ – the sort of arctic condition that will impose a strain on the very best plumbing.

Basically it is all a matter of using the right size pipes, properly lagged where necessary and making sure that the whole system can be drained easily. The latter is especially important for those who are going to be absent for the winter. Turning off the water main will restrict flooding to the amount of water still contained in the pipes if a pipe bursts, but the pipes will still be full of water, which can expand when frozen and cause the damage. Turning on all the taps after the mains have been turned off will empty most of the pipes, but not those below the level of the lowest taps. Therefore a drain-off cock should be fitted as near as possible to the lowest point of both hot and cold pipes. Ideally this should have somewhere to drain into conveniently; a length of hose leading to the nearest drain out into the street or garden will help here.

Where the system is remaining in service for the winter, the risks are less because the house will presumably be kept warm. Where pipes are at risk from the cold, however, efficient lagging is very important. Modern, split tubes of lagging make this job a lot easier than it used to be.

The last two items are the type of vital thing likely to be completely ignored by the 'cowboy' plumber. Also, as is often the case, if his equipment doesn't run to pipe bending, each bend will mean another joint and each joint represents another potential weak spot. In some cases his skills might not even run to soldering and if compression joints are used throughout, the price of materials will rise astronomically.

Apart from hazards posed by the elements, incorrect pipe sizes can cause a few headaches such as: clattering when a tap is turned off too quickly (many modern taps cut off the supply very abruptly with the flip of a single lever), starving of water at one point when a tap is turned on at another (this is the one likely to freeze or scald anyone using the shower at the time) and inadequate water pressure two or three floors up, to name but a few.

If there ever was a case for making sure a tradesman was the genuine article, it applies especially to the plumber, whose training and experience will have made him familiar with all the problems and given him an intimate knowledge of what is required for each facet of the job. His estimate might be more, but it is more than likely the final account will be less than that of the 'cowboy', for a better job complete with guarantees.

Supply
Each region has its own water authority (*service d'eau*) which will have an office in any medium or large town.

Those buying a property without a supply of any kind (which is rare, but still possible when buying a derelict ruin) will, for a price depending on the location, i.e. the distance from the nearest water mains, be connected to a supply and issued with a meter on demand.

This does not normally apply to apartments. Due to the rising cost of materials and installation, the supply is now limited to one per building. I use the word normally, because different water authorities have been known to bend the rules from time to time. It is worth asking, they can only say no. Mostly then, if there is already a supply to any particular building, it will be up to the individual owner to connect up pipes from this leading to their own apartment, installing a private meter – around 250 francs (approximately £25) from DIY superstores or plumbing specialists – to keep a check on individual consumption so that the bi-annual water bill can be apportioned between each user.

All this sounds very simple and straightforward and in the case of a purpose-built block of apartments, probably would be. There would also be, no doubt, a management of some kind to take care of it. One would not, however, expect to find a derelict flat in such a place. In most cases it will be in a very old building which has been divided and sold off in a random fashion over many years; each flat will be freehold, with no organization to look after communal problems and, worse still, is likely to consist of other flats which have long-term inhabitants who have been there since the days when the *service d'eau* installed individual meters.

This can pose a very real problem for the new owner without a supply, because it will entail plumbing into someone else's supply. They will not only have to run the risk that you might not pay, or be slow to pay your share of the bill, but also have to suffer the inconvenience of your plumber boring holes through walls or ceilings to make the connection. After that, he will become responsible for working out who pays what.

All in all, it will not be surprising to find that other owners are unwilling to co-operate.

On the other hand, even if you do the responsible thing and go along to the *service d'eau* to find out the unit price (*prix unitaire*) of water, remembering you want the TTC (*tout tax compris*) price, so that you can work out from your meter reading how much to pay, plus a division of the standing charges and additional taxes, there is no guarantee that the person you are connected with will pay the bill. If he doesn't, or leaves it too long, the supply will be cut off.

Obviously everyone needs water, so the bill will normally be paid to keep it flowing. This sort of hitch is only likely to arise when the apartment of your shared supply has been let, with no clear understanding of who pays the bill, or the owner has gone off on a long holiday just before the bill arrives (through *his* letter box). However genuine the excuse, it won't help you at the time and the only way to have the supply turned on again is to go to the *service d'eau*, pay the whole bill and hope to recover the other share later.

If this happens once, for a valid reason, there is probably no need to assume it will be a regular headache. If it becomes so, however, a visit to the *service d'eau* will usually find them quite willing to have the bill transferred to your name and address. After all, their main concern is getting payment and sending out their operatives to cut off or re-open a supply costs them money. If you have to resort to this course of action though, have a plumber rearrange the main taps so that if the other party refuses to pay their share you can cut them off as a means of encouragement. Whilst such action may not be completely legal, it usually achieves quick results. If it happens that the other party is being supported by social security, it can have the effect of getting that department involved and achieving a pattern for future payment.

A more pleasant aspect is that should your neighbour be absent during a freeze up, you will be able to minimize possible damage by shutting off his supply.

Wells and Bore Holes
As housing developments gather pace in various parts of France, town water is becoming more widely available, but there will still be remote areas without any form of piped supply, or where the connection to the nearest water main would be far too costly.

In some cases an established old building will have a well (*puits*), which might or might not be usable. If the building has been long neglected there is a good chance that the well water might be contaminated by falling rubbish, dead animals and so on – especially where there is no capping. It is possible, however, to have it drained and cleaned by a specialist, who may be found through the *mairie* or *Department d'Equipment*. In any case it is obligatory to have the water analysed annually. The nearest laboratory will carry out this task at a price predetermined by the government. Laboratories are to be found in most towns, where they also do blood and other such tests for the local doctors. If there is an intention to install a septic tank, it should be at least 35 m from the well.

A short term solution to water supply is to install a water tank as high up as possible and fill it with cans of water collected from the nearest town tap (these are still plentiful in most towns and villages and will usually say *non potable* if the water is not fit for drinking).

The long term solution is to have a bore hole (*forage*) drilled. This is a highly specialized operation, but quite usual in remote areas, so locating a firm who does it will usually only be a matter of searching the yellow pages or asking at the *mairie*.

A rough guide to the cost (1991) is around 150 francs (approximately £15) per metre for a hole of about 17cm in diameter. In addition to this, the liner which has to be added is around 70 francs (approximately £7) per metre and then there is the submersible pump and the cost of electricity to run it. The pump always goes at the bottom of the bore where it is able to raise the water at considerable pressure. For some complex scientific reason, a surface pump can only raise water about seven metres, however powerful it is. The actual drilling is quite impressive to watch, as the large bit slowly grinds its way downwards at a rate of around one metre per hour.

Obviously the cost is directly related to the depth at which the water is found and it is as well to know that the drilling company are responsible for sinking the bore hole, not for finding water and therein lies the nub of the problem. A visit to the *Department d'Equipment* will reveal maps of underground streams and water tables etc., but they are not always accurate, so many borings may bear no fruit. A water diviner, if he is good, will be able to pinpoint the presence of underground water, the probable quantity and even the number of litres per hour it could deliver, but these gifted people are not usually able to guarantee their predictions, and have been known to underestimate the depth by forty or fifty metres. There is little choice, however, so the thing is to sound out the local knowledge to find the best diviner.

(Incidentally, a lot of people are naturals at this without being aware of it. Try holding the bottom edge of a steel coathanger between thumbs and index fingers just hard enough to keep it horizontal and walk over a known but buried water pipe. The hanger will swivel downwards if you have whatever it takes.)

Piping

Now that lead pipe is being phased out, the supply from the *service d'eau* to the meter will normally be in 25mm bore black polyethylene. Inside the building it is most usual to change to copper. All French copper piping is metric; the sizes, i.e. 10/12 mean 10mm inside diameter and 12mm outside. Thus the first figure is the important one to look at when considering whether there will be an efficient flow to all points.

The sizes used should not be less than the following specifications:

ITEM	DIAMETER
WC (*cabinet*)	10mm
Wash basin (*lavabo*)	12mm
Bidet	12mm
Shower (*douche*)	14mm
Bath (*baignoire*)	14mm
Kitchen sink (*évier*)	14mm

This applies to both hot and cold pipes, and means that the supply to the hot tank and the outlet from it should not be less than 14mm pipe.

Despite this, it will be noticed that many houses are plumbed throughout with 10mm pipe, which, being smaller and lighter, is cheaper than the larger sizes, but will prove to be a false economy.

Copper pipe to be buried under concrete, under a floor, for

example, or embedded when passing through a thick wall, should be encased in a PVC conduit, which should be a loose fit. The type used to protect electric wiring will suffice and is readily available. This will allow for any expansion.

Where piping is being layed under a floor, or anywhere else that will become inaccessible later, it is better to use the type bought by the roll. In this way joints will not be necessary for those stretches, thus eradicating potential weak spots.

Unrolling the pipe calls for a definite technique if one isn't to end up with multiple kinks which become almost impossible to straighten. The secret is to place the roll upright, stand on the end of the pipe and roll it away from you (wearing soft shoes). Advance step by step along the pipe as it unrolls. With a little practice it will come out almost straight.

This kind of pipe is quite soft, and bends of about 15cm in diameter can quite easily be made, but do this in short lengths of about two inches at a time to achieve a graduated bend. Trying to do it all in the same place will flatten the pipe and constrict it.

Those who favour piping on the surface for easy future maintenance will find that buying the harder pipe in straight lengths will make it easier to end up with a neat job. The type of pipe clamps specially made to hold two pipes will help keep them nicely parallel.

PVC piping for both hot and cold supply is slowly overcoming traditional prejudice and being more widely used. It will be found in most of the DIY superstores in 14mm, 16mm, 20mm and 25mm diameter. All the usual joints, bends and reductions are available, including a type coupled to a brass nut for attachment to a meter, tap or other threaded item. The joints are stuck together with a similar glue to that used in PVC drainage plumbing, but with a higher specification to withstand mains pressure. This pipe might find favour with DIY plumbers who don't feel up to soldering.

Regarding soldered joints, it is difficult to find the pre-soldered type in France – they are almost exclusively the capillary type to which the solder is added once hot enough. For those wishing to have a go for the first time, the golden rules are: shine up the pipe ends thoroughly with wire wool or fine sandpaper, don't be mean with the flux, heat up both ends of the joint at the same time (or all three if it is a 'T') until the flame turns green. At this stage the solder will be sucked in to the joint as you touch it against the hot copper.

If your property already has a water system installed and it suffers from the kind of clonks and clatters that wake up the household when used at night, this can be alleviated by fitting one or more expansion chambers (*antibelier*) at strategic points. This usually means near taps or toilet reservoirs (cisterns). They are designed to absorb some of the powerful hydraulic effects of water coming to a sudden stop when a valve closes too abruptly.

Those whose property is in a region of very hard water will inevitably get problems from calcium/limestone deposits known in France as *calcaire* or *tartre* which clog up the pipes and tanks. In these regions it is advantageous to have a water softening filter in the supply. Filters are also available to combat bacteria and foul smelling water. The latter is often caused by a special anode in the hot water tank put there to discourage *calcaire*. When the tank is in regular use there is usually no problem. It seems to occur more in holiday homes unused for months at a time. Tanks of recent manufacture seem to have overcome this problem.

Drainage Plumbing

As most evacuation is done with PVC piping these days, each joint being stuck with a special glue, it is generally easier to work with than copper, but to drain efficiently, both the sizes used and the slope (*pente*) must be right.

PVC is most widely available in grey, but some of the larger stores do it in white or tan, which may suit some decors better.

Recommendations are as follows:

ITEM	DIAMETER	SLOPE	IN CENTIMETRES PER METRE
Toilet	100mm	2-3 minimum	4-5 preferable
Bath	40mm	5 minimum	8-10 preferable
Shower	40mm	1 minimum	4-5 preferable
Bidet	32mm	1 minimum	2-3 preferable
Kitchen sink	40mm		

Washing machine 32mm
Dishwasher   32mm
Wash basin   32mm

The last four items are not so critical for slope. Dishwashers and washing machines pump out the waste and the height of the average sink means that the flow of the water is accelerated by the initial fall. With the bath, shower and bidet, especially the bath, the steeper the slope the better.

In most houses the above angles are not usually difficult to obtain, especially as it is usually possible to drop down through the floor, but an apartment is denied this advantage and so achieving quick, efficient drainage will call for some ingenuity.

It will help if the bath, WC and shower are sited as near as possible to the main evacuation point. Sometimes it is necessary to raise the bath up a few centimetres. Precious centimetres can be gained by using the thickness of the exterior wall to create a downward slope to the outside and also by coupling the various evacuations (bath, sinks, WC, etc.) outside, rather than at interior floor level, as is often done.

Insufficient slope of the bath or shower drainage will manifest itself in two ways: taking a long time to drain and water bubbling up through the plug hole when a nearby sink is emptied. The system as a whole will also have a tendency to become blocked up more easily by hair and other matter that would be washed away by faster drainage.

Rodding eyes fitting into the system at strategic points of toilet and smaller waste pipes will greatly facilitate the clearance of blockages. Alternatively this can sometimes be done by pouring a litre or so of *chlorhydrique* (hydrochloric) acid down the plug hole or toilet basin, but this can also weaken joints as too much can destroy the glue.

Main Drainage
Main drainage and sewage is also the responsibility of the *service d'eau* who supply the water. Most towns and villages have an efficient network of sewers these days which provide an outlet or evacuation for each house.

Unfortunately, the same rules that apply for the

installation of water meters and supply, count for evacuations as well, i.e. one per building. So, once again, the apartment bought without a sewage outlet is going to be a problem for the new owner, who, if aware of the fact, should make the provision of an evacuation system a condition of purchase.

It may seem a remote possibility to buy an apartment that lacks any form of drainage, but this is not uncommon, in fact, as many top floors subsequently divided off and sold were part of the apartment below when it was all one house. Frequently, toilets, bathrooms, kitchens and all other plumbed-in services were on the lower floors – the upper levels being used for bedrooms or just storage.

Where the apartment below has a sewage pipe fitted externally, branching into it is not usually much of a problem (with the owner's consent of course). Often, however, it is either internal or, where the walls are thick, it runs down a vertical channel inside the wall. This may often be located by tapping around the wall to find the hollow area.

In a lot of old town and village property the services have been updated but not the sewer. Many of these places, regardless of size, have had just one toilet which may have then been used as a general evacuation point for subsequent plumbed-in items on the floors above.

Whether or not this works depends largely on the siting of the original toilet and the condition of the drainage channel running under the house. It can appear to work, in other words, everything runs away, but there might be other problems such as damp and smelly walls which were not previously recognized as being a sewage problem.

A lot of these drainage channels are merely stone slab bases and sides with a joint every 50cm or so. Over the years the mortar will have decayed, which means that every joint is a potential leak. Most of this leakage just seeps into the ground beneath the house, but where the channel runs beneath or alongside a wall the dampness will inevitably rise up.

Often, the top of the channel is under one row of the floor tiles, so its location can be easily found by tapping and listening for the hollow note. Hopefully though, it will not be necessary to lift the row of tiles and cause a lot of damage to what is possibly a magnificent old floor. Whether it is necessary or not will depend on available space because the cure of this problem is to insert a liner of 100mm or 130mm PVC piping. (100mm will do for all but large houses where numerous toilets are being installed.)

Where the original toilet was (or perhaps still is) at the back of the house, especially in the case of terraced property, it is likely that the channel ran from there, in a straight line out into the street (often under the front door) where it will slope down and curve round in the direction of the main sewer. All the liner has to do is to carry the sewage clear of the house by a metre or so. Thus if there is space in the toilet to insert a four metre length of the PVC pipe (it is sometimes necessary to cut a hole through the wall through which to slide the pipes) it can then be followed by others, gluing each joint well, until the pre-measured length is sufficient. This PVC liner then becomes the main drainage for the house and all services are subsequently plumbed into it.

There might be variations, of course. It could be that other services are planned for the front of the house, in which case at least one tile will have to be lifted to 'T' into the new liner. For this purpose, however, it would need to be close to a wall where the pipe from above could be neatly boxed in.

Before inserting the new liner, the old channel should be thoroughly rodded out to make sure it is clear, especially where it is to remain covered for most of its length.

This simple and inexpensive operation should cause the damp wall to dry out within a few weeks. The time will depend on the outside temperature, the ventilation, the thickness of the wall, etc. If the damp continues and it is a party wall, it is possible your neighbour has a similar old channel soaking into the other side! With luck, they might be interested to know the cure and have a new liner fitted. Needless to say, the new liner should have a conveniently placed rodding eye to facilitate the clearing of any future blockages.

It has been known for experts on rising damp to be called in, theorize about underground springs, wells, streams, etc. and suggest all sorts of expensive injection treatments to cure this particular problem. Where advice is sought, it should always be from a local builder, architect or drainage plumber well versed in the type of property concerned.

Rural Main Drainage

When buying property in a fairly remote part of the countryside, there will be those who are out of reach of the nearst village sewage system or who find that the price quoted for a lengthy connection by the *service d'eau* is far too high for their budget.

In this case the alternative is a septic tank, which is quite a common system in rural areas. The chances are that the property, unless derelict, will have one already, but there are still plenty which, for countless years, have relied on an outside 'privvy' and a hole in the ground.

Septic tanks and their ancilliaries – inspection chambers, leach drains, filters etc. – are available from most builders suppliers, the whole assembly not normally costing more than 6,500 francs (approximately £650) (1991 price). (See diagram.)

Unlike a cesspit, which is merely a collector which needs regular emptying, the septic tank is actually a sewage treatment system which, with the addition of enzymes and certain bacteria, breaks everything down naturally so that the overflow from the leach drain pipes is just water. One in good repair shouldn't smell at all, and only needs emptying about once every two years.

Certain precautions are necessary to keep it working well; for instance, household bleach (*l'eau de javel*) or any product containing it will destroy the microbes essential for its efficient operation. A list of chemicals to avoid introducing into the sewage system will normally come with the installation instructions. If you have inherited a tank with no list, ask at the builders' suppliers. Once the working organisms have been destroyed, the tank will have to be emptied and regenerated with new enzymes etc.

Don't let the necessity of having a septic tank put you off buying a place in the country, a minimum of maintenance will keep it working so well that it will be no more trouble than being attached to the mains.

Water Heating

The majority of water heaters, especially the instant ones that work on gas or electricity, are the same as those available in the UK and so don't need any explanation here.

Typical Arrangement for a Septic Tank

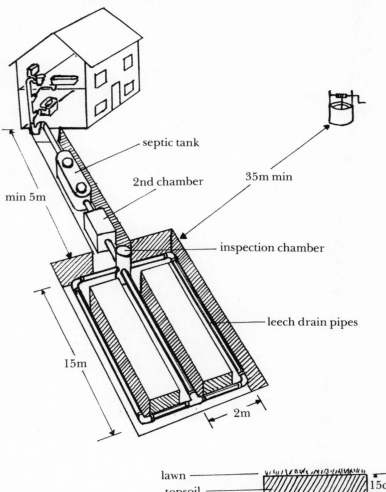

septic tank

2nd chamber

35m min

min 5m

inspection chamber

leech drain pipes

15m

2m

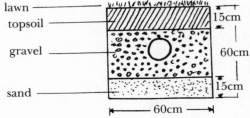

lawn
topsoil
gravel
sand

15cm
60cm
15cm

60cm

The main item that differs from the UK is the *chauffe-eau electric à accumulation*, to give it its full title, although it is known all over France simply as a *chauffe-eau* or *cumulus*.

Unlike the UK system of a header tank feeding a main tank which gravity feeds the hot taps, the *chauffe-eau* works off mains pressure, and so can be sited anywhere convenient, including the basement.

One of its best features is the built-in insulation (it is really two tanks, an inner and outer skin with the gap filled with polyurethene foam) which makes it extremely efficient. Once heated to the temperature set on the thermostat (about 60°C is considered a good average) it will retain the heat for a considerable period, making for economic use of electricity.

They are available for horizontal or vertical fixing, but apart from a few designed to sit on a specially made stand, the normal method is, by virtue of the built in brackets, to hang them on a wall. As they are quite heavy even when empty, and very much more so when full, it is essential to get the fixing bolts really well secured. This is sometimes a problem with old walls that might not be completely sound.

One method is to remove a stone and fix in a wooden pad at each point, liberally covered with nails to grip and well plastered in. If the stonework is sound, 12mm expanding bolts will be effective, but if you are in any doubt, a back-up, belt and braces system will save whatever disasters might result if it falls off the wall (and some have). Should it have a tendency to do so, it will fall forward (even two bolts will stop it dropping vertically). A precaution against this happening would be a bracket or suchlike fastened to an overhead beam and resting against the top/front of the tank, or a joist which would support the bottom/front edge if necessary.

Bear in mind that with a vertical tank, which is the most common, the thermostat, electrical connections and water inlet and outlet are at the bottom, so it should not only be mounted high enough to get at this region easily, but also for the security valve to drain into a convenient waste pipe.

This valve (*groupe de sécurité*), mounted on the inlet side (marked blue, the outlet red) is absolutely essential, as it copes with any expansion which might otherwise split the tank. It drains into a special syphon (water trap) similar to the type found under any sink.

Most manufacturers give a seven- or ten-year guarantee, which is for the tank only, not the thermostat, heating-element or safety valve which will be covered for up to two years.

When selecting a *chauffe-eau*, it is a mistake to get one that is too small. Sizes range between 30l. and 300l. and if it has to supply a bath, it should not be less than 150 litres. The rest depends on the average number of people in the household. Either your plumber or the store you buy it from should be able to advise.

The electrical connection should be on a separate circuit, using 2.5mm^2 or 4mm^2 wire. For further safety and convenience a fused on/off switch should be mounted near the tank. The circuit calls for two live wires and an earth, but, like most French appliances, has no marked position for positive and negative as this is considered unimportant.

Should the thermostat be heard to be 'clicking' in to activate the heating element too frequently, when no hot water is being run off at the time, it is either faulty and needs checking, or the tank and heating element is too caked up with *calcaire* and has become inefficient. Renewal might be the obvious cure, but it is possible to open it up and clear out the offending sediment. The procedure is to first drain the tank (turn off the mains and open the safety valve) turn off the electric power at the fuse box, disconnect and withdraw the thermostat, having first removed its plastic cover, undo the hexagon headed bolts which seal the inspection plate and remove the plate.

The hole is large enough for an arm to enter. It is not unusual to remove a bucketful of *calcaire*. After this, reverse the procedure to re-assemble.

Ideally, the longest run of pipe between the *chauffe-eau* and the furthest hot tap should not be more than eight metres. It should never be installed where likely to be affected by frost, i.e. an uninsulated and unheated outbuilding or loft.

Plumbing Check-list

FAULT	ACTION
1. Noisy pipes	Fit expansion chambers
2. Lack of water pressure	Piping too small or blocked with *calcaire*. Could also be supply problem, consult *service d'eau*.

3. Water starvation (when another tap is turned on)

Piping too small. Bear with the inconvenience or install larger bore pipes.

4. Sour smells or sewage smell

Check water traps under any item seldom used, such as a bidet. If the water evaporates the trap will cease to function. Run some water down plug hole to fill it up.

5. Foul smelling water

Could be anti-calcaire anode in *chauffe-eau*, or bacterial problems. Fit filters as advised by store or plumber.

6. Slow drainage

(a) Blocked piping. Try plunger, rodding out or acid.
(b) Insufficient slope on drainage pipes.
(c) Drainage pipes too small.

7. *Chauffe-eau* boils

Thermostat faulty or adjusted too high (over 60°C causes rapid *calcaire* build-up).

8. *Chauffe-eau* won't heat up water.

Thermostat set too low. *Chauffe-eau* needs clearing of *calcaire* and maybe new heating element.

9. Burst pipes in winter.

Insufficient lagging. System doesn't drain properly when absent. Fit drain-off cock.

10. Septic tank smells

Microbes destroyed by bleach etc. Empty and regenerate as per instructions.

A magnificent carved basalt doorway unfortunately marred by
the drainage pipes added three hundred years later

An interesting mixture of styles and tiles in Dreux town centre

Ornate roof ridges on a town house in Montlucon, near Clermont Ferrand

The sort of very narrow alley to be found in many old towns and villages

A converted *remise* showing how the original entrance has been modified to make a front door

Entry through what
appears to be a front door
sometimes reveals an
attractive courtyard

14 Central Heating

Anyone visiting the south of France in the summer may be forgiven for thinking that central heating (*chauffage central*) is an unnecessary luxury. In fact, winters can be extremely cold, even if for a shorter period than many other parts of the country (the north and the mountain regions have prolonged cold weather).

The type of heating you choose to install will depend on the use of the property. For short stays in or out of season, some form of instant gas or electric heating may suffice. Only experience will tell.

If the decision to opt for central heating is taken, it should be made as early as possible. If it is left until the renovation is complete, your home will once more be turned into a battlefield of dust and rubble in the process of boring holes for all the pipes to pass through. As with the electric and water installations, the sooner you have this done the better. It is quite likely anyway that the plumber doing the latter will also be able to install the central heating at the same time, which should be much cheaper than having the two done separately.

The type of central heating chosen may be a matter of personal preference and the range available differs very little from that found in the UK, i.e. coal/wood, gas and electric (in some of the warmer regions these will be backed up by solar panels).

Electric is usually the easiest to install, requires the least maintenance and has a great variety of heating points, i.e. oil-filled radiators, convectors, night-storage heaters which run on a cheap tariff etc. The annual cost is likely to be higher than other systems and there is always the risk of power cuts.

Gas is clean, quite economical and efficient. Where there is town gas available the installation (the actual boiler) is fairly small and easily mounted on a kitchen or bathroom wall. Gas, however, is not available everywhere, which means using a *citerne*, a large, oval container some 2m long and 1m in diameter in which to store the gas. These are hired from such companies as Total, Antargaz, etc., and can be refilled by tanker on demand.

The problem here is one of space. They have to be outdoors and at least three metres from the house. It is possible to have them all or partially buried in an underground chamber to make them less of an eyesore. Obviously this system is only suitable where sufficient land is available.

Oil (*mazout*) is widely used in France, and a variety of boilers (*chaudières*) are available. Also clean and efficient, the boiler is best sited in an outbuilding or scullery and so is more suited to rural property or large houses. Unfortunately oil has become a victim of international disputes and so is sometimes in short supply and with fluctuating prices.

Coal/wood is also best suited to rural areas and is usually the cheapest form of heating. The main disadvantage is the daily chore of reloading and ash clearance. Coal and wood burning stoves are much more sophisticated than they used to be, making for greater efficiency and economy.

For any system needing regular yearly maintenance, the installation is best carried out by a local firm, who are on the spot should problems occur. They should also be able to advise on the most suitable system for the locality and for your particular needs.

Whichever system you choose, some form of back-up is advisable in the form of a portable gas or oil heater to cope with power cuts.

Good insulation is extremely important to save wasted power consumption. Figures have been produced that show that, for example, an apartment of $110m^2$ will need 26kW to heat it if uninsulated and only 18kW if insulated. Similarly a two-storey house needing 32kW uninsulated needs only 22kW when insulated. This will include double glazing, roof insulation, etc.

Ventilation both at floor and ceiling levels is also very important to improve the air/heat circulation and vent humidity outdoors.

15 Electrical Installation

Supply

As it mostly runs overhead, electricity is easier to connect than water, and so the EDF (*Electricité de France*) will quickly install a new supply to any property, on demand, including apartments, with a 220 volt supply (110 volts went out some years ago).

What they will need to know is how much power you require, as there are several different choices. They will then be able to tell you roughly what the installation will cost and when they will be able to do it.

Those who have reason to be cynical about 'promise dates' from large national organizations are very likely to be pleasantly surprised by the fact that the engineers will probably turn up not just on the right day of the rendezvous, but frequently within minutes of the pre-arranged time. I don't doubt others will have had different experiences, but after several involvements with the EDF I have had nothing but courteous efficiency.

Buyers of old property are most likely to find any existing installation hopelessly inadequate for modern requirements, so if in doubt it is better to have the whole lot stripped out and renewed. It will be safer as well; overloading old wiring is one way of starting electrical fires. The EDF will come and check it out if asked.

The French work on a different system to the UK; there are no ring mains, for example, so most things work off individual fuses, and, as a result, fuse boxes contain more fuses. It is similar to what we know in the UK as a spur system. Whether it is better or worse is a matter of opinion, but I can confirm that a well installed system does not seem to give any problems.

It is a very common occurrence for a new owner of old property to be constantly frustrated by what they feel is a faulty trip switch (*disjoncteur*), frequently cutting off the supply for no apparent reason (the red button is for testing that it works, the black pressed to restart it). In fact, one of the first things to check is the electricity bill, to see what the standing charge (*l'abonnement*) is. It might be that the supply is the lowest and thus cheapest category, which is only sufficient for lighting and minor appliances. The new washing machine is likely to trip the switch every time the fridge comes on.

At the time of writing (1991) the smallest supply has a monthly tariff of about 12 francs (approx £1.30) whereas the next one up is more like 33 francs, which won't be affected by the washing machine, but it might be if the dishwasher is switched on at the same time!

There are four main choices of supply as follows:

1. 3kW will run a fridge, TV, lights, vacuum cleaner, power tool, etc.
2. 6kW will run all of the above plus *chauffe-eau*, washing machine, dishwasher, electric cooker, but only one of the latter three at the same time.
3. 9kW will provide enough power for all items above, but two of the large items can run simultaneously.
4. 12-36kW (several choices in between.) For a home with all the latter plus central heating etc.

If in doubt as to which supply to choose, it is quite simple to add up the total requirement for your appliances, but having done so, it is seldom necessary to be supplied with that amount of power. For example, it would be very rare for an electric cooker to be operating on all four hot plates (*plaques*) at the same time as the oven, and even if this was the case it wouldn't necessarily be at the same time as the washing machine and dishwasher were working, plus all the lights, TV, etc. Thus your 8kW cooker (*cuisinière*) will seldom be using more than 4kW and you don't need 6kW to work a 3kW washing machine (*lave-linge*) and a 3kW dishwasher (*lave-vaiselle*) unless they are used simultaneously. The following formulas may be of use:

Cooker	4kW
Washing machine OR dishwasher	3kW
Lights and other small appliances	1.5kW–2kW
Supply needed	8.5kW–9kW

Cooker OR Washing machine OR dishwasher	4kW
Lights and other small appliances	1.5kW–2kW
Supply needed	5.5kW–6kW

If you start off on the smaller supply and then install, for instance a 2kW *chauffe-eau*, it can easily be stepped up to the 9kW or 12kW if other things are added. This will be done free of charge, but, of course, the standing charge will rise accordingly. Above 12kW it might be necessary for the EDF to run larger cables to your meter, in which case there will be a small charge (about 250 francs or £25) rising to about 1,500 francs or £150 for a really heavy supply of 24-36kW.

Each supply has a higher standing charge, after which you pay for the metered consumption. As in the UK there are special meters available for those wishing to take advantage of off-peak rates (for hot water, night storage heating, etc.)

To have the incoming power raised is often just a case of the engineer putting a larger capacity fuse in the trip switch, but in some old towns where the average home is supplied with, say, six kilowatts, stepping up to 12 or above might not be possible.

There is usually a minimum charge for a new supply, after which the price goes up by the metre. Thus a connection in a town or village centre will be cheaper than further out in the country, where it might involve new pylons or poles.

Costs for this can be in the region of £1,000 per pole from the nearest EDF supply to your property, which is why it is sometimes better to be independent and opt for the installation of a diesel generator (*groupe électrogène*). If you have lived in the property without an EDF supply for four years, the *mairie* is obliged to pay 50% of the cost of connection by way of a grant. (This might vary from region to region, but should be enquired about.)

The procedure is to visit the nearest EDF office. They will

then send out one of their men to survey the situation and give an estimate. If you agree the price a deposit of 50% is immediately payable before the work starts.

There is something of a mystery as to why connection to electrics is so costly, whereas connection to a telephone, which involves roughly the same operation, is around £25 regardless of distance. The EDF will supply power to the meter, which is their property. They will, if asked, supply a trip switch as well, but this will be yours, and charged for on the next bill.

You (or the electrician) will need to install a positive and a negative 6mm² wire from your fuse box to where they decide to mount the meter. In the case of an apartment, they usually agree to connect your 6mm earth wire as well, otherwise it will be your responsibility to install an earth strap (A steel rod for hammering into the ground which has a connection for the earth wire).

Installation
It is possible to do your own installation, but it will have to be checked out by the *Consuel* (*Comité National pour la Security des Usagers de L'électricité*), who, if satisfied, will issue an attestation of conformity which is necessary before the connection can be made. This can take up to a month to obtain and the EDF will tell you how to go about it. (The electrician, if you use a registered one, will already know.)

Specifications for the various circuits are as follows:

CIRCUIT	WIRE SIZE	FUSE
1. Lights	1.5mm²	10 amps
2. Power points	2.5mm²	16 amps
3. Washing machine	2.5 or 4mm²	20 amps
4. Dishwasher	2.5 or 4mm²	20 amps
5. Cooker plus oven	6mm²	32 amps
6. Chauffe-eau	2.5 or 4mm²	20 amps

Where the size of the equipment varies the size of wire depends on the size and power of the appliance. For example, a *chauffe-eau* of 50 litres will run safely off 2.5mm² wire but one of 150 litres needs 4mm².

With all the larger appliances on their own individual circuits, the small things will get plugged in to the various power points. Hopefully you will have persuaded the electrician to adopt your suggestion of two or three conveniently placed points per room, rather than just one, which will subsequently get festooned with adaptors and extension leads.

The first thing you will notice about French wall sockets is that they are small, and have either two holes or two holes and an earthing pin. None of them have on/off switches. The plugs have either two pins, or two pins plus a hole for the earthing pin in the socket to marry up with.

The thinking behind this is that the sockets with just two holes are for small appliances only; wall lights, TV, Hi-Fi, radio, small power tools etc. All these items, bought new, will come with a two pin plug. Items over 3,500W will be supplied with a plug with a hole for an earth pin, which should make it obvious that it is not for plugging in to what might only be a lighting circuit.

It is recommended that all sockets to be mounted over a floor surface should be of the type with an earthing pin. This is because the floor could become a conductor of electricity when wet.

Sockets are best kept out of bathrooms anyway, but it is actually illegal to mount one within 2.5m of a bath or shower tray. A razor point should be at least one metre away.

Although frequently done, it is not the best scheme to have all the power points on one spur (i.e. all originating from the same fuse) and all the lighting on another. Apart from the fact that indiscriminate plugging in of appliances could cause overloading on the power circuit, it also means that if the fuse were to blow on the lighting circuit the whole place is plunged in to darkness. Naturally it is potentially dangerous to grope around a fuse box trying to replace the offending fuse in the dark, not to mention the very real possibility of tripping over something on the way.

Two, well planned circuits for each, lights and power will obviate both of the above problems. Of course, there is no limit to the amount of circuits you can install for each purpose, but more than necessary will mean ending up with an awful lot of fuses.

Specialist electrical suppliers sell little stick-on symbols to identify each fuse, which is a good practice to adopt when there are so many to choose from. Your electrician will probably do this anyway, for his own benefit as much as yours, in case he is called back at a later date to sort out a problem or add another installation. If you are doing your own, however, and can't find the symbols, it will pay to label them in ink or some recognizable way rather than to rely on memory.

There are a bewildering amount of fuses available in France, varying enormously in price – some with lights, others with their own little trip switch and some which just take a small cartridge-type fuse. The latter add to their own confusion as different makes take different sized cartridges.

The more expensive type are said to give better protection to the circuit, but the cheapest (cartridge) type are still acceptable to the EDF, so 'you pays your money and you takes your choice'. Just stick to the same make to keep it simple and buy at least one spare set of cartridges for each capacity (i.e. 10 amp, 16 amp, 20 amp and 32 amp).

Despite long-term rumblings about Euro-standard colours for wiring, it is still sold in red or brown for the positive, blue or black for the negative and only the earth is now almost always a combination of green and yellow. All the above are acceptable, the EDF being more concerned, and rightly so, that the sizes are right.

A truly amazing amount of wire gets swallowed up in the course of a new installation. It is not abnormal to get through 100m of each colour wiring up an apartment. Considerably more can be used in the case of a house on several levels. It is much more expensive buying short lengths, so, if buying your own, don't be afraid to take advantage of special offers which are often available in the DIY superstores on coils of 100m and upwards. The cheapest (but still perfectly adequate) kind is the single strand rigid type bought in individual colours, but even if you buy positive and negative or ditto plus earth in one outer sheath, all should be run through a conduit for protection.

Conduits are available in rigid PVC tubes, plus all the usual joints, bends and 'T' pieces, normally in three-metre lengths, or in flexible PVC bought in coils of various lengths, the longer of which contain a thin steel wire which is for pulling the electric wiring through (which, as experience will tell, is a lot easier than pushing it).

The rigid conduit is more expensive, but looks neater when surface mounted and is easier to get the wire through. The flexible type does not need joins and is good for running through places which will be out of sight and for weaving a twisty path amongst stonework to reach a switch or wall light where it is to be buried beneath the mortar before repointing.

Although colour coding is very necessary for identification in circuitry, it will be noticed that quite a few appliances will only have the earthing point symbolized. In most cases it is irrelevant which way round the positive and negative are attached unless polarity is important, as it is in fluorescent lights and some electronic items. In these cases it will be clearly marked.

It is important for all bathroom fixtures to be 'earth bonded', i.e. hot and cold copper pipes to all points (sink, bath, bidet, etc.) should be connected up to the earthing system.

These are just the basics. A glance around the big stores will reveal such highly sophisticated things as infra-red switching, where lighting and other appliances can be activated by a beam, radio signal or a command unit such as those used for TVs. The lover of modern gadgetry will not be disappointed with the selection available in France.

The most important thing is to start planning the positions for lights, switches, power points as early as possible, so that the necessary wiring runs can be laid before major work covers everything up and makes it impossible, impractical or at least very time consuming and expensive. In a big restoration job, the electrician should be one of the first to be called in so that the holes and channels he has to make will be covered up in the normal course of rendering or plastering. If he has to attend to all this himself, his charge will naturally be higher.

As a final word, never be tempted to install a larger than recommended fuse. The fuse is there to protect the circuit, which, if overloaded and allowed to carry on functioning will overheat and eventually catch fire. If a fuse fails frequently and electrics are not your thing, an expert should be called in to check why it is happening.

Electrics Check-list

PROBLEM	ACTION
1. No current at all	(a) Check trip switch by pressing black button. If no result:
	(b) Check with a neighbour. If their electrics are working ring EDF.
	(c) If they are not working, it could be a strike, lightning (in which case the supply will soon be restored), overhead supply cables blown down, etc.
	(d) Electricity bill not paid.
2. Trip switch cuts current	(a) Check for overload if new appliance recently fitted. If black button stays in with new appliance turned off, apply for extra supply.
	(b) Short circuit – call electrician.
3. Lights go out or other apparatus stops working	(a) Check fuse and replace if necessary. If it happens often the fuse is either the wrong size or the appliance is too powerful for the circuit. If in doubt, get expert advice.
4. Appliance won't work	(a) Check fuse.
	(b) Check for bad connection (once the electricity has been turned off).
	(c) Call in expert to check fault in appliance or exchange under guarantee.

16   Gas

There are two types of gas supply available in France: natural gas supplied by the GDF (*Gaz de France*) and butane or propane supplied in bottles and tanks by various private companies.

The GDF will be found in the same office as the EDF (*Electricité de France*), which is where you should go to make enquiries about a connection, or the servicing of existing installations.

GDF gas is available in most towns, but if your property is outside the town it will depend how far you are from the nearest gas main. Obviously it is not economic to go through the costly exercise of laying pipes where there are only one or two potential customers.

Where the main is close at hand, the price of connection will be in the region of 1,500 francs–1,800 francs (approximately £150–£180), unless the GDF are having one of their periodic promotional campaigns, at which time it could be considerably cheaper.

A supply is piped to a gas meter in your home which measures cubic metres and fractions of, but the four proposed rates, depending on your requirements are assessed in kilowatt/hours per year:

1. Base less than 1,100kW per year (gas cooker only)
2. B0.   1,100–7,300kW per year   (gas cooker plus water heater, bath heater or radiator)
3. B1.   7,300–17,000kW per year (gas cooker or bath heater plus radiator, or free-standing or wall-mounted water boiler and radiator)
4. 3GB   17,000–30,000kW per year (cooker, hot water and central heating)

If in doubt, advice is free from the GDF, whose gas is non-toxic and therefore no use whatsoever to potential suicides. Provided there are no distance problems a connection can usually be made quite quickly, i.e. within a few days, but if the pipe has to cross someone else's land, the GDF have to get planning consent from that person and the *mairie*, which could take time.

Bottled gas is either in the form of propane or butane, which are similar in power and price, but where they are to be subject to frost it is best to use propane. Butane freezes up when the temperature is around freezing point; propane is supposed to keep flowing down to about $-10°C$, which is good for all but freak conditions. Obviously both will give better service indoors or in an insulated outbuilding.

Most qualified plumbers can fit gas installations and also advise on the type of container best suited to your purpose, which vary between portable bottles and huge horizontal cylinders which arrive by specially adapted lorry and crane.

These large containers are usually rented on a contract basis, but the portable bottles have to be purchased initially, after which the empty can be exchanged for a full bottle for the current price of a refill. The supply is controlled by a regulator, which must be either for propane or butane but appliances normally work on either without modification.

Whereas the large storage containers have a pressure gauge to give an indication of the contents, the small bottles don't, so it is better to have a dual linkage system and two bottles. In this way the empty can be taken away to exchange while the back-up bottle keeps up the supply. Without such a precaution they have an uncanny way of running out halfway through cooking for a dinner party.

While Butagaz is probably the most widely available in France, other popular makes are Totalgaz, Elf Antargaz, Primagaz, etc. All of which are in portable bottle form and are sold at garages, supermarkets and local village ironmongeries.

Always make sure you keep the receipt which comes with the initial batch of bottles (they are around £25 each) and that way you will be able to get your money back if you decide to go over to another form of power.

17 Tiling

Floor Tiles

Tiling (*carrelage*) should be regarded in the same way as gloss painting – a finishing touch, the final surface, only to be applied when all the preparation underneath has been done. Bad preparation will seldom take long to make itself evident.

Floor tiles (*le carrelage sol*) generally have a tough life which they will stand up to very well, but not if they are laid on a bad foundation. If the under surface moves for reasons of softened mortar, rotten or badly supported boarding, or if it is so uneven that there will be hollow areas under the new tiles, they will very soon start to crack up. Chapter 9 deals with this particular problem and its remedies.

Assuming then that the floor is covered with either a new concrete raft, or unremarkable old tiles on a sound base, both surfaces are likely to need a final levelling before laying the new tiles. In the UK a self-levelling screed would be used. In France this is called *autolissant* or *ragréage*. It is mixed, as per the instructions, with water until it is the consistency of cream, and spread on to the surface with a long float, like the type used for plastering, but longer preferably. It then finds its own level.

As with all things, the surface should be clean, dry and free from grease or dust. *Ragréage* is only designed to be applied in a thin coat of between 2mm and 10mm, so normally the coverage should be about 1.25kg–1.5 kg per square metre. Any deep depressions or irregularities should be pre-filled, using a finely sifted sand and cement mix. If this, or the concrete raft or old tiles are especially prone to being dusty, and consistent attempts to remove it are not successful, it should first be treated with a *resine d'accrochage* (available from builders suppliers in various brands) which goes on like milk and stabilizes the surface.

The *ragréage* will dry in about ten to sixteen hours, depending on the ambient temperature, but should be left for thirty-six to forty-eight hours before tiling.

Most brands of *mortier colle* (a tile glue with a mortar base) are suitable for interior and exterior application, but this should be confirmed on the packet. Most types are mixed with water at a ratio of around three to one (three powder, one water). Coverage depends on the size and thickness of the tiles, the larger and heavier the tile, the more 'bedding' it needs, so for very small mosaic tiles it will be between 1.4kg–2kg per square metre. Medium-sized tiles (15mm x 15mm) up to 3kg per square metre and very large tiles, especially those with embossed lines or patterns on the underneath, up to 6kg per square metre. It is important to work out the likely quantity of *mortier* (or *ciment*) *colle* you will need, and, as usual, the larger sacks are much cheaper pro-rata.

The adhesive (*mortier* or *ciment colle*) should be spread with a toothed spreader making sure there will be no gaps underneath. (Hollows could subsequently fill with water and expand when frozen, cracking the tile.)

The choice of tiles in the large suppliers is so great as to be totally bemusing unless you go with a very clear idea of what you want in size and colour. Obviously this is best left to the individual, but whatever you choose, don't make the mistake of over-economizing, especially when for use outside. Poor quality tiles will very quickly lose their good initial appearance when they start suffering from frost or hard-tipped shoe damage. Most good quality tiles are made to withstand frost and their surface is very durable.

Terre cuite, always very popular for use in old buildings as it looks so traditional, is more or less unique amongst tiles in being unglazed. Because of this, the surface is porous until treated later, so it tends to be very prone to staining from tile adhesive and grouting (*joint*). A lot of this can be wiped off with a dry rag (never a wet one, however good the initial result looks, as this will spread the staining around the tiles). Anything left can be cleaned off afterwards (taking the usual precautions, e.g. rubber gloves and goggles) by giving it a scrub with hydrochloric acid diluted four (water) to one (acid). When clean and dry the tiles can then be painted with as many coats of linseed oil and white spirit (equal parts) as are necessary. (The tiles will eventually stop absorbing the mixture and can then be polished.) Failure to apply this treatment before the tiles are walked on, risks staining the initial, absorbant surface with something that can't be removed.

When laying ready glazed tiles, beware those that are too glossy as they tend to be very slippery.

Tiles in *terre cuite* are never regular, i.e. never exactly the same size. Because of this the grouting gap needs to be larger than average to allow for differences between adjacent tiles. 10mm is quite normal instead of the usual 2mm to 4mm.

Rooms in old buildings are never regular either, which makes a well planned floor plan essential if the tiling is to end up looking good.

Irregularities can sometimes be minimized by diamond or herring bone patterns, but if they are going to be straight lines, the best are those which start at right angles to the main entrance to the room and go in a straight line across it. If the tiles are lined up with one of the walls, and this happens to be at an obtuse or acute angle with the entrance, the effect will look crooked or even be disorientating when you enter the room.

A competent tiler (*artisan carreleur*) will already know this, but it won't hurt to show him a plan of what you want before he starts. While he might not want to be told how to do his job, he should have no objection to adopting your design unless he can show you that his would be better.

Ideally, the first line of tiles to be laid will lie astride a line drawn from the centre of the doorway to the far wall. Never make the mistake of tiling across the doorway to the left- or right-hand wall and then laying another line down that wall. It will never be a right angle, so the result would be subsequent tiles all needing to be ground down to fit, or gaps which get increasingly wider towards the other end of the room. With a true line of tiles down the centre line from the doorway, the tiles can work towards the sides and end of the room with geometric precision, and the cutting needs only be done around the edges.

The only variation from this plan should be (if necessary)

in the bathroom or kitchen where there is to be fixed furniture. It looks a bit odd if the floor line doesn't run parallel to the tiles. Good planning is vital for a good end result.

Another problem that often arises when tiling over an already tiled floor is caused by the inevitable rise in height. With thin floor tiles this can sometimes be successfully faired in with a slight chamfer at the change of levels, but thick tiles are likely to cause the sort of insignificant step that people are likely to trip over. It may be possible to carry on the new level throughout one whole floor, in which case it will probably only be a matter of shortening each door a few centimetres. The placing of the new level of tiles needs careful thought as small steps are dangerous, especially when the surface is all the same colour. So, if there is no alternative, a break in the colour can help, or a wooden trim – something to make the step as visible as possible.

Those intending to do their own tiling will find all the necessary tools for scoring and cutting normal tiles adequate, but for *terre cuite* or other very thick tiles it will be best to hire a special disc-type cutter. An angle grinder with a stone-cutting disc will do the job, but great care is needed to keep the cutting disc vertical. If it begins to lean over as the cut gets deep, it tends to jam up, often with dramatic results – broken discs, tiles and windows, etc., not to mention injury to people.

Much less exciting is the proper tool, with its mobile disc mounted to ensure a ninety degree cut, or adjusted for an angled cut if required. The hire will be more than an angle grinder, but possibly cheaper in terms of possible damage.

With any sort of cutter of this type, hot dust and chunks of tile are bound to be a hazard, so safety goggles are vital. The damage that could result from injury to an unprotected eye is too dreadful to risk.

Aids to help the regularity of laying come in the form of little plastic crosses, which can remain in place at each corner. Sizes vary between 1mm and 8mm. They are called *croisillons*. Straight lines chalked on to the floor can be a great help with the first few rows in either direction.

Wall Tiles

Wall tiles (*le carrelage mural*) are thinner, lighter and easier to cut with ordinary tile tools, and need just as much planning and preparation for good results, if not more so, because they are frequently placed all around a room and to look good the lines must remain level.

In fact, the word 'level' is the key to successful wall tiling. A spirit level is probably the most important tool, coupled with a plumb-line for the verticals.

Just as very few walls are straight in old buildings, very few floors are level, so the first move when planning wall tiling is to find out which is the lowest end, make a mark the height of the chosen tiles, 15cm for example, and using a long spirit level, draw a line to the other end of the wall. In this way, for the top edge of the fixed tiles to coincide exactly with the line, an increasing amount will have to be removed from the bottom of each tile. It is a lot easier to remove small amounts from a tile than to cut small wedge shapes to fill the gaps if the line had started at tile height the other end.

Where to start is always difficult when there are windows, reveals, worktops, splash-backs and taps to be worked into the scheme neatly. It is often a good idea to experiment with a 'dry' line of tiles to see what looks best. There are books dealing solely with this subject which have more space to explain techniques in detail.

It is mostly a question of verticals and horizontals and this is the side of it that often needs working on in old buildings, which are usually conspicuously lacking in both. Wall tiles never look good when mounted on an uneven surface, so if the surface cannot easily be smoothed, it is sometimes quicker to line it with plasterboard (which tiles stick well to) or make a thin inner wall from 40cm x 20cm x 25mm honeycomb bricks. It can be made vertical at the same time.

If the wall is smooth and sound (tiles won't stick to damp or loose plaster, so these problems should be dealt with first) but leans back beyond the vertical, as so many walls do, the same technique can be used with a plumb-line as was done at the base with the spirit level, i.e. the plumb-line should start from one tile's width at the top. Each tile will therefore have to be cut down to fit between the plumbed line and the corner. Marking the vertical as well as the horizontal base line will help to determine where to start the bottom row so as not to end up with a very small width of tile to cut at one end.

Round holes for taps and other pipes to pass through can be cut with a string saw (*scie vilebrequin*). This is a bit like a fret saw, but the blade is round in section and embedded with industrial diamonds to give it a stone-cutting capability. If the hole is to be in the middle of a tile, drill through with a masonry drill large enough to insert the blade and then re-hook it to the saw frame. It takes a while, but is much neater than splitting the tile.

If a work surface extends over a washing machine, leave a little clearance, or when the machine is loaded out of balance it will vibrate and shake the tiles out.

As with floor tiles, the choice is astronomic in France with tiles and designs to suit all pockets. The catalogues often contain good ideas like matching table and sideboard tops laid in a diamond pattern and tiles being used to disguise a ledge hiding pipes etc. The glossy magazines and books in local libraries always have pages showing the completed job, where artistic minds have produced all sorts of interesting and innovative ideas.

18   Woodwork

In any old French building wood plays a major role in the construction, fittings and décor, from beams to balustrades. A visit to one of the large, national joinery stores (*menuiseries*) will reveal an impressive display of doors, windows, shutters, spiral and other forms of staircases, garden gates, garage doors and so on.

Most things, including the staircases, come in kit form for home completion to keep the prices to a minimum, but the quality is generally high in comparison with some other forms of mass production. Many items can be bought in either soft or hard wood, to suit different decors and pockets.

Although geared towards the rapidly expanding French DIY market, many builders buy here as well – a sure reflection on the value. In many cases it is cheaper to shop at one of these places than to buy the wood and make the item yourself, unless your time is your own and you have plenty to spare.

Another method of buying joinery items, a little bit more labour intensive, but with the chance of more authenticity, is to use items which have been recovered during demolition work. Some demolition contractors just dump or destroy everything in the quest for speed, but the more enterprising keep the re-usable items for selling later. This is a good source for beams, doors, old wooden staircases, etc. Some things will be half price or less, some more, depending on the basic condition and present availability. For example, near Beziers there is such a contractor with a huge, two-storey barn, packed to capacity with all sorts of goodies. Whilst searching for a new front door, I came across a magnificently carved set of double front doors. They were very large, about eight feet high, each door three feet wide and superbly made, as things were in the first part of the last century and in sound condition. The asking price was about £1,500. There were also a lot of more suitable doors for around £40, but it just goes to show what you can find with diligent searching as you get to know the neighbourhood and ask around.

Finding re-usable doors, windows, etc. on the local tip is very much a matter of luck. In the early days of a renovation job, visits will be fairly frequent and so the chances better. The local totters, of course, where the size of the town reflects the amount being dumped, spend most of each day there scavenging for scrap iron and other metals amongst the arriving rubbish. They will not be interested in woodwork, so there will be no conflict of interests. In fact, for a small inducement one of the regulars could be persuaded to put aside items for you, if you can make it clear what you want. It has been done.

When buying timber there is the usual big price difference, as in the UK, between buying it sawn or prepared. It is also noticeable that some of the prepared woods in DIY stores are of very mediocre quality, with joins at regular intervals. Although these are machine made and bonded, and thus probably adequate for most internal jobs, these joins can be unsightly where wood is to be clear varnished rather than painted. If you have the facilities it is often better to buy it rough sawn and plane and sand it yourself, or have a local *menuiserie* do it for you.

All the usual woodworking glues are available in France, plus some specialized resorcinal and epoxy types. If these are not easily found in your nearest store though, and you are making something for outside installation, it is best to buy the glue from the nearest boat-builder or chandlery shop.

Fastenings of all types are found in plentiful supply. In this respect the DIY superstore being a virtual replica of its UK counterpart.

France has its own brands of wood-treatment solutions, the best known being Fongix, Xylophene and Lassailly which have a triple function: 'fongicide, insecticide, hydrofuge' (fungicide, insecticide, sealer). All these are very thin liquids and thus suitable for using in a pump up insecticide spray normally used in the garden. This will give much better saturation and reach the parts that brushes cannot. Some of these are colourless *incolore* and some have a brown tint. All declare themselves to be non-toxic, but a good face mask will avert a lot of coughing and goggles will keep the eyes from stinging too much. The best saturation comes from adjusting the spray to a fine mist, which gets everywhere, so protect the floor and anything that can't be removed with plastic sheeting. Some boat chandlers now do a very useful range of plasticized, disposable overalls which are ideal for this sort of job.

After the treatment is dry (two or three applications won't hurt) you can then proceed to stain it (as the treatments are colourless). The same manufacturers make the stains, also containing preservation and anti-mite ingredients, in all shades from very light pine to very dark ebony, with a satin or matt finish.

For exterior application, the major companies also do microporous finishes which allow the wood to breath, but protect it against too much moisture absorption.

Given good ventilation and regular treatment, wood has proved to be amazingly durable over the centuries. It normally only runs into trouble when allowed to come into contact with rainwater and conditions of bad ventilation, a situation that encourages the growth of fungus and subsequently rot. Both this and wood-boring mites can be easily controlled with today's materials allowing us to co-habit with this pleasant, warm, living substance.

19   The Kitchen

Those seeking a new kitchen (*cuisine*) and equipment will have no problem in France, where every industrial estate (*zone industriel*) on the outskirts of any large town will have at least one large warehouse specializing in the very latest types and styles with a range to suit all budgets. Apart from the specialists, all the large household furniture and electrical equipment stores (*electro-ménager*) have large sections devoted to kitchens, cookers (*cuisinière*), fridges (*frigo*), freezers (*congélateur*), microwave ovens (*four micronde*), etc. as do a lot of the hypermarkets and DIY superstores. This is BIG business. The French housewife, it seems is every bit as keen to keep up to date as her British counterpart.

A lot of the stores are geared to the DIY market, so the assembled cabinets in the showrooms bear little resemblance to the 'flatpacks' you collect from the *entrepôt* round the back.

Even with the cheaper kitchen furniture the quality tends to be quite good, with adjustable legs to cope with uneven floors and the backs of the cupboards set in a few inches so that some of the chassis can be cut away to fit over pipes, or closely up against walls that are not vertical. Assembly instructions are usually in several languages including English, and the number of tools required are kept to a minimum.

Those wishing to have the kitchen fitted for them would do better to buy from the kitchen specialists rather than the stores, as they will have their own fitters or ones that they can recommend. Trying to find fitters privately could get complex as trades in France don't overlap much, so it is possible that a carpenter, a plumber and a ceramic tiler would all have to be involved.

It seems to be taken for granted in these days of convenience that however old the house, the kitchen can be space age. Apart from some of the rural districts, there are not many households still cooking on wood/coal burning ranges, although, where there is space, these very attractive old stoves double up nicely in the winter for cooking as well as heating. It also costs nothing extra to have the kettle on for a hot drink at any time of the day. Diesel, gas and electric versions are still available new (at a price) but the old ones can still be found occasionally at a *brocante* (antique/second-hand shop) a *depot de vente* (a sale-room for second-hand household goods) a flea market (*marche de puce*) often on Sunday mornings in some towns – France's answer to the car boot sale.

In all these places it is also possible to find taps, sinks, fridges, kitchen units and all the other items thrown out when a new kitchen gets fitted. The *petites annonces* (the postcard sale board by the supermarket check-out) and the local free advertising papers should be scanned as well.

The old type of white pottery or stone kitchen sinks were always very practical, mostly being large enough to pile the washing up in and accommodate a plastic bowl. Most of these had an integral draining board as well. They, too can be found in the above places if they weren't smashed in removal. I would think very carefully about scrapping these sort of things if you are lucky enough to buy a property equipped with them, just to replace them with something no more useful and with a much shorter life expectancy. After all, fashion being what it is, they will probably be an integral part of the post space age kitchen.

At least it is possible to get traditional styles in new kitchens which, with a balanced blend of tiles mean that work surfaces and wood trim can be made to look very pleasant.

DIY kitchen builders aiming for the traditional look should always use large section 'chunky' timber. Cabinets based on a solid pine framework (at least 7cm x 8cm) with old style (new) panelled doors and the right type of tiles fastened to the chipboard work tops (let in so the tiles are flush with the pine) can be very effective. Pine shelving should be at least 25mm thick. No old kitchens were delicate.

Those who have found old doors from the tip or elsewhere will find that even if the bottom is decayed, there might be panelled sections that can be cut out to make cupboard doors. These not only look authentic, they are authentic.

Tongued and grooved parquet (floor planking), which can usually be bought in four grades (the more knots the cheaper) makes better looking shelves in cupboards than chipboard. The latter, however, is more suitable for sticking tiles to.

20 The Bathroom

Depending very much on the age of the property, and whether it is in town or country, it will either have no bathroom at all, just an outside privvy, or a footprint-type toilet in the cellar (*cave*) which a modernist of the past has turned into a dual function facility by adding a shower unit! In other words, nothing that measures up very well to present day thinking on hygiene and efficiency.

It is very likely then that part of a room will have to be walled off to create a bathroom that never existed before.

A large room with a marble bath enthroned on a central plinth is very impressive if there is space to spare, but a lot of town and village centre houses are decidedly lacking in floor area, so careful planning is vital to fit everything in.

In actual fact, not all that much space is needed for a fully fitted bathroom, at least some of which can be fitted into space which would normally not be very valuable (see diagram). The bathroom in the diagram is wrapped around a communal stairwell, taking up very little of the actual room, but still has adequate standing space with a full-size bath, sink, bidet, toilet and *chauffe-eau*.

By using a hip bath or a shower, even less space would have been used. Also, the bidet, since the advent of the shower, is no longer a vital piece of bathroom equipment and could have been left out altogether.

When installed on the top floor, or loft (*grenier*) under the slope of the roof, it is worth bearing in mind that headroom is only necessary for a bath on the side you climb in and out of. Advantage can often be gained by siting it against the wall and having the sink and toilet in the higher parts.

Shower basins (*bac à douche* or *receveur*) come in two types: *à poser* or *à encastrer*. As the names suggest, the first

Bathroom Wrapped around Communal Stairwell

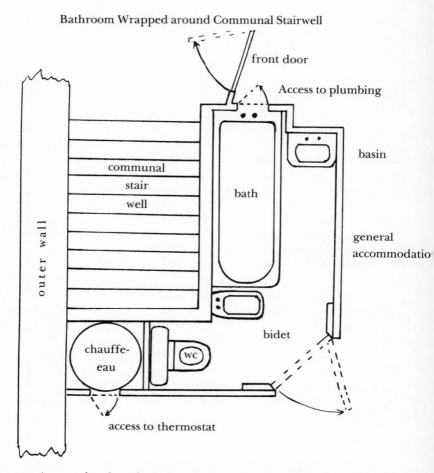

type is merely placed on the existing floor surface, and is thus the easiest to install. The second is designed to be built in, and therefore has the advantage where headroom is limited, as it can be let in to a suitably formed hollow and fitted flush with the floor tiles, to step down into.

The first type can be bought with side drainage, which may be a must for an apartment, but with the second type the drainage usually has to go through to the floor below, unless it can exit into a communal stairwell without offending the neighbours.

As, in either case it will be difficult if not impossible to get access to the waste or water trap, it is important to get the type which lifts out from the top, to clear the inevitable hairs that will pass through its grill.

Amazingly, cast-iron baths which are far and away the best type because they don't creak and groan when you move and have that nice solid feel, are often scrapped in favour of plastic ones that come in fancy colours. They can therefore be found second-hand, in good, cleanable condition provided the last owner didn't leave it out in the rain with the cast iron legs in it. This leaves rust marks that resist every known cleaner.

Whichever bath you choose, it is important to have good access to the water trap and taps for future maintenance. Often though, this would interfere with the line of the tiling on the side or end. One way of getting around this problem is to have the tap and trap end up against a wall and have the access in the wall itself, below bath level through a small, opening door. This can give better access than from the side without interfering with the décor.

With the tiling and grouting done around the bath or shower, it is still necessary to run a bead of silicone sealing plastic around the join to avoid potential damp problems.

For maximum watertightness, it is always a good plan to embed the side(s) of a bath or shower basin into the wall, i.e. cut away the plaster until the edge of bath or shower tray is resting against the brick or stone. In this way the tiles will overlap the edge and any splash should run naturally and harmlessly where it is supposed to go. Still use the silicone though, splash can travel uphill.

It is advisable to install all fittings involving masonry drilling before applying the silicone seal, as the fine red dust from the tiles or bricks causes discolouring which is almost impossible to rectify.

Toilets are not usually a problem where they can be sited near the main evacuation point. The further away they are the more difficult it is to get the slope sufficient for the waste pipe. Where a convenient siting is impossible, or where it might even have to be below the level of the main drainage, the answer is to get the electric type. These have a small treatment tank below the cistern for the evacuation to connect with and a pump which can lift the waste up to 2.5m through a small bore pipe, which, unlike the normal 100mm type, can easily be concealed or disguised.

Cisterns, where space is very limited, also come in very shallow depths or are corner-fitting types.

Special promotional offers from the big stores are always limited to the mega-mass-produced standard bathroom equipment with a choice of white or white.

Lack of good ventilation gives rise to unsightly mouldy patches in the corner of the ceilings and walls, and should be thought about when choosing the site for the bathroom. If an opening window is not available, trunking (available in flexible types or 100mm PVC will suffice) to the outside and an extractor fan will solve both this and odour problems.

21 Security

I have a French friend locally who never locks his door, even if he intends to be absent for days at a time. His attitude, unusual among the normally very security-conscious French, is based on the theory that a burglar, finding the door unlocked, would immediately presume someone is there and so go and ply his trade elsewhere. Or, if he comes in anyway, at least his entry won't have caused a lot of damage.

It isn't a new theory, no doubt others feel the same way, although I very much doubt if their insurers would agree. In any case just imagine how sickening it would be if the burglar forced his way in through a window, not knowing about the front door!

Probably it is a matter of luck, but there can be no doubt that the homes of foreigners, known to be unoccupied regularly are a special risk.

Whilst stolen goods are occasionally recovered, the normal thing seems to be that the victim reports his loss to the *gendarmerie*, or the *police national* (not the *police municipal*) who ask them to make a statement (*compte rendu d'infraction*) to make it official, after which the onus is put on the insurers who, unless you have been to make a report to the police, will probably not pay out.

First then, make sure your insurance (*assurance*) covers you for the value of the property you might have had stolen.

Assurance offices in France are quite numerous, and mostly seem to be agents, but affiliated to one of the big companies. Local *assurance* is probably better for local problems.

The other way to look at the problem of theft is crime prevention. There are several things which make it harder to break in to a house such as good, strong shutters, for example, where the top and bottom studs are firmly in place to receive the end hooks of the *espagnolettes*. A well fitting shutter made from sound timber which locks properly would take a good deal of strength, and make a fair amount of noise in the course of being forced.

Some burglaries, of course, take place in broad daylight when the shutters would normally be open. The owner might not bother to shut them just to go on a brief shopping trip. Furthermore, some people don't like shutters anyway, so the alternative is an iron grill set into the brick or stonework with the bars close enough so that even a very small person couldn't pass through. Most *assurance* companies insist on this. This very effective barrier, if made in a traditional, decorative style, needn't be reminiscent of prison bars, which are not. With those on the ground floor windows and glazed doors, any burglar looking around the district for an easy job will hopefully continue his search elsewhere.

There are special locks available for the front door (probably the only entrance in a town or village dwelling) which have a triple function. Apart from the normal one of shooting a bolt in to its slot in the frame, they also shoot one into the top of the frame and one into the floor. It would take something akin to a battering ram to dislodge one of these. Other locks have hi-tech keys, like torpedos with fins. None of these is very cheap, some costing over £200, but where your home is at risk, this isn't so much.

Some *assurance* companies insist on at least two separate locks on the main door. It will pay to query this, or they might decline to pay out on a claim.

Having made the windows and doors secure, try to put yourself in a burglar's shoes. Are there any other weak points? Balconies or roof windows can be vulnerable, is there a tree that would give an agile person easy access to upper windows? Is the roof itself secure? I have an acquaintance who lives in the country outside a village who lost a garage full of expensive power tools and building equipment by an entry forced through the roof. A pan tile roof is especially vulnerable on this score. The tiles themselves are usually only fixed at the top (the ridge) so it would be very simple to lift a few, take up the slabs they are resting on and expose the joists. The latter would even be a help in swinging down to floor level. Once inside, of course, most doors can be easily opened. A vulnerable roof, therefore, should have a strong internal lining, such as 19mm chipboard put up with long screws, or some other suitable barrier as a deterrent.

Burglar alarms could, I imagine, make a lot of would-be burglars think twice, as they make a lot of noise when activated. Whether or not you fit one, it is still not a bad idea to display a *villa piège* (literal translation: house trapped) sign in a prominent place.

Time switches working lights and a radio from time to time can help to make it look as though someone is there. As can a trusted neighbour, by hanging some of their washing on your clothesline, and removing letters etc., which might otherwise look conspicuous if left sticking out of the letter box for too long.

Guardienage is a good idea for large, isolated places, although it is very important that references should be well checked out. With this system, someone, often a couple, come to live in your house whilst you are absent. Some get paid, others are happy to do it for the comfort of having mains electricity and hot water for a few months. The latter are often boat owners (if the property is near a canal, river or the sea) who would otherwise have a great deal less in the way of facilities, while waiting for the spring to continue their voyage. Similarly, those touring in mobile campers are often happy to stop for the winter.

22 Gardens

As the French are very keen on their gardens, there is no shortage of garden centres, sometimes called *pépinières*, selling everything from lawn sprinklers to swimming pools and a great variety of trees and shrubs.

This section, therefore is more a matter of what you can and can't do on your own patch.

For instance, any trees or shrubs likely to grow more than two metres in height must be planted at least two metres inside your boundary. Shrubs which don't grow as high as two metres can be planted within 50cm of the boundary. Officially, any fruit on your tree which overhangs the dividing fence into your neighbours property belongs to the neighbour. There are, however, certain exceptions which provide grey areas and work for solicitors. All in all it would be much better to reach an amicable agreement with the neighbour.

There are strict regulations concerning the storage of anything inflammable, toxic or foul smelling. This is not necessarily illegal, but should be discussed with the *mairie*.

It would not be permissible to start up a dog kennels or keep pigs next to any other existing house.

Swimming pools, garages and garden sheds are not necessarily going to get automatic planning permission, neither are mobile homes or very large caravans that might block a neighbour's view.

As in the UK, you will not always be allowed to cut down an established tree, even if it is blocking your light.

Consultation with the *mairie* is the best way to avoid problems with the authorities.

23   Health

Building work is not without its hazards, even for those who are regularly occupied with it, but for those whose business life forces them to be relatively inactive, the risks and dangers are doubled.

Apart from the unaccustomed strain of lifting bags of cement or plaster, joists, beams or large stones, new fridges and so on being very likely to cause ruptures and back problems, too much wielding of a heavy hammer to knock out old mortar can very quickly blister skin more used to a pen or a steering wheel.

The sunshine, especially in the south, makes it very tempting to take off shirts. The sun can be very deceptive when you are working, especially if there is even the mildest breeze. By the time you notice the soreness it is already too late. Work for the next few days will be agony, as it will with blisters or a bad back.

It all sounds very obvious, probably patronizing as well, but there are so many ways you can put yourself out of action, possibly for as long as your working holiday. Over-enthusiasm can kill. It is my wish in writing this book that you should enjoy the project you are embarking on, not end up in hospital.

There are many ways of making life easier, such as spooning the cement out of the sack into some of the buckets you have collected. A bucketful is already none too light, but a sackful is asking for trouble. Levers, jacks and hoists can help shift heavy things.

Protect your skin with sun-block cream and your hands with heavy duty gloves. Wear strong shoes rather than sandals or flip-flops as the feet and toes are especially vulnerable to very painful injuries.

I have never liked wearing hats, but being knocked unconscious briefly by a fairly small piece of falling masonry while holding a ladder for someone made me think again.

If you are resident in the UK and only in France for up to six months at a time, remember to visit your local DSS office before leaving to get an E111 form. They might need a few days notice. This is the reciprocal health agreement between most European countries which entitles you to get a refund on any medical treatment necessary while abroad. It is meant to be seventy per cent but VAT and various other taxes are subtracted before the seventy per cent is awarded. Even so, fifty per cent is a lot better than nothing on a possibly expensive course of treatment.

The system is for a visit to a doctor (a general practitioner is a *medicine general*, sometimes *généraliste*). You will be asked to pay for the consultation (usually between £9 and £14) but he will give you, apart from the prescription for the pharmacy, a sheet of paper called a *feuille de soin*, with his charge recorded on it. Take this to the pharmacy (presuming you need medication of some sort) and they will transfer the sticky labels from the medicine boxes on to the form. The form must then be signed (by the husband, in the case of husband and wife, even if it is the wife receiving the treatment) and taken to the nearest C.P.A.M. (Caisse Primeur Assurance Maladies), from where it will work its way through to the UK and you will eventually receive a cheque. Hopefully, it will not be necessary.

Should you be unlucky enough to need urgent hospitalization for reasons of serious accident or illness it pays to know that the fire service (*sapeurs pompieres*) run an excellent, free ambulance service. Dial 18 (no money or phonecard necessary) and they will arrive swiftly, give first aid on the spot where needed and take you to the nearest suitable hospital (most vital as some hospitals and clinics are not equipped with casualty departments and will have to turn away some cases). They will also radio ahead to have everything ready for your arrival.

Appendix 1: Aids to Restoration

Material	Features
Resine d'Accrochage	Can be added to mortar to help make a dust-free surface, or painted on afterwards for same effect. It is also painted on very shiny surfaces (e.g. tiles) to make new tiles, paint etc. adhere better.
Ciment Fondu	Provides hard, smooth, resistant surface. Ideal for garage floors, making (moulding) mesh reinforced inspection cover lids etc.
Ciment Prompt	Hardens in minutes. Good for bedding in hinge fastenings etc. into stone or brick. Fills cracks in stone, fibro-ciment drainpipes etc.
Mortier Rapide	Quick setting, also good for bedding in hinge pins (usable in thirty mins) fixing ridge tiles and edge tiles, flashings, window frames, fixing posts in position, etc.
Mortier Batard	High adherence, good for rendering difficult walls, even if damp. Resistant to cracking, and can be used for all roof work.
Mortier Refractaire	Heat resistant to 1,200°C. Good for lining chimneys, joints in barbeques, fire bricks, etc.
Accelerateur de prise et antigel	Speeds up cure of concrete, mortar, etc., and makes resistant to frost damage.
Hydrofuge de Masse et Plastifiant	Makes mortar adhere better (i.e. for rendering).
Durcisseur de Surface anti salt-petre	For painting on stonework, mortar or concrete. Clears salt-petre deposits, destroys fungal growth, lichens etc., and hardens surface.
Anti mouses, algues, lichens	For cleaning off fungal growths and making surface better for painting.

Barrière anti humidite des remontees capillaires	Rising damp wall injection treatment.
Impermeabilisant incolore de surface	Colourless liquid to make stone, brick, mortar, etc. impermeable
Barrière anti-humidité de surface	Same as above but can also be used on wood and metal.
Ragreage or Autolissant	Self-levelling surfaces.
Enduit de lissage et de rebouchage	For filling cracks in plaster or creating a patterned surface (as Artex in UK).
Enduit colle Polyvalent	For taping and filling joints in plasterboard. For sticking (in blobs) plasterboard to wall when dry lining. For sticking insulation materials to wall or ceiling. For sticking together plaster wall blocks (*carreaux de plâtre*).
Briqueteur	For sticking together honeycomb type *terre cuite* bricks on internal walls.

Appendix II: Bricks and Blocks for Internal Walls

Terre cuite (honey-comb type)	In a range of sizes starting from 25mm thick. Mostly 40cm x 20cm in width and height. Jointed with Briqueteur, and can also be used externally.
Béton Cellulaire	Grey, lightweight (hollow) concrete blocks, mostly 40cm x 20cm. Thickness starts around 100mm and jointed with mortar.
Carreaux de Plâtre	Lightweight tongued and grooved plaster blocks. Large range of sizes. Jointed with Enduit Colle Polyvalent. Can be cut with ordinary wood saw.

Appendix III: Types of Nails, Screws and Hooks

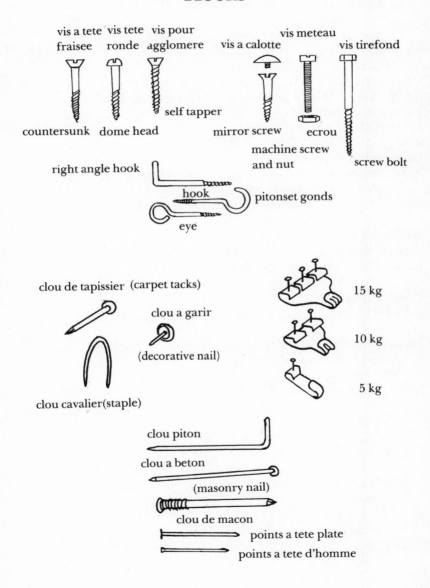

vis a tete fraisee
vis tete ronde
vis pour agglomere
vis a calotte
vis meteau
vis tirefond

self tapper

countersunk
dome head
mirror screw
ecrou

machine screw and nut

screw bolt

right angle hook

hook

pitonset gonds

eye

clou de tapissier (carpet tacks)

clou a garir
(decorative nail)

15 kg

10 kg

5 kg

clou cavalier(staple)

clou piton

clou a beton
(masonry nail)

clou de macon

points a tete plate

points a tete d'homme

Appendix IV: A Selection of Suppliers

DIY stores
Castorama (over 100 branches throughout France)
Mr Bricolage (also many branches throughout France)
Gedimat (as above)
OBI (as above)

General building materials
MBM (many branches throughout south and west)
Union des Materiaux (as above)
Gedimat (many branches throughout France)

Wood materials
(doors, windows, staircases etc.)
Lapeyre (55 branches throughout France)

Plumbing Materials
Brossette

Furniture and electrical stores
Conforama (throughout France)
BUT (as above)

Appendix V: A Selection of Agents, Consultants and Property Papers

Agents
Alouette French Properties
Tel: 01798 872876
Fax: 01798 875865

Bill Estate International
(Brittany, Perigord, Languedoc)
Tel: 00 33 99 68 08 93

Burgundy Property
(Burgundy region)
Tel: 020 8341 1773

Chateaux Leisure Properties
(south-west region)
Tel: 020 8673 9289

Property Consultants
Bull & Bull (Solicitors)
4 Castle Street
Canterbury
Kent CT1 2QF
Tel: 01227 456300
Fax: 01227 764315
(Also in Paris and Lille)

Briarose
223 Route National
665000 Prades
France
Tel: 00 33 68 05 00 40
(south-west region)

Margaret Haskins
La Vigneronne
15 Avenue Pierre Sirven
34530 Montagnac
France
Tel: 00 33 67 24 11 55

F.G. de L. Rutherford
197 Knightsbridge
4th Floor
London SW7 1RB
Tel: 020 7581 1978/2178
(throughout France)

Property Papers
Dordogne Telegraph
7 Place d'Armes
24290 Montignac
France

Focus on France
Tel: 020 8542 9088

French Property News
21 Cromfort Way
New Malden
Surrey KT3 3BB
Tel: 020 8942 0301

Appendix VI: Application for Town Planning

 cerfa
N° 10543*01

MINISTÈRE DE L'ÉQUIPEMENT,
DES TRANSPORTS ET DU LOGEMENT

DEMANDE DE CERTIFICAT D'URBANISME
(Article R.410-1 du Code de l'urbanisme)

Notice N° 50237*01

Répondre à toutes les questions de l'imprimé en écrivant à la machine à écrire ou au stylo à bille noir.
Seul le premier feuillet de liasse est à remplir. Les autres feuillets sont autoreproductibles.
Écrire en appuyant fort sur une surface dure.

1 – COMPOSITION DU DOSSIER DE DEMANDE

1 - 1 - Le dossier de demande de certificat d'urbanisme se compose de :

● *L'IMPRIMÉ DE DEMANDE*

● *QUATRE PLANS DE SITUATION :*
Le plan de situation est établi à une échelle comprise entre 1/5000 et 1/25000 de format 21 x 29,7 cm. Il doit comporter :
- L'orientation ;
- Les voies de desserte avec l'indication de leur dénomination ;
- Des points de repère permettant de localiser le terrain.

Vous pouvez utiliser :
- Un extrait du plan d'occupation des sols de la commune,
- Le plan du tableau d'assemblage cadastral qu'il est possible de recopier en mairie,
- Ou une carte géographique ou touristique dont l'échelle convient.

● *PLANS DU TERRAIN :*
Le plan du terrain est établi à une échelle comprise entre 1/500 et 1/5000, si possible de format 21 x 29,7 cm. Il doit comporter :
- Les dimensions des côtés ;
- La voirie de desserte ;
- L'emplacement des bâtiments existants.

● *UNE NOTE DESCRIPTIVE, éventuellement (voir ci-dessous)*

1 - 2 - Le certificat d'urbanisme peut être demandé pour quatre raisons différentes. Le dossier varie suivant le cas. Lorsque la demande porte sur plusieurs objets un seul dossier doit être fourni.

OBJET DE LA DEMANDE	COMPOSITION DU DOSSIER
a) Demande en vue de savoir si le terrain est constructible ou non (article L. 410.1.a. du Code de l'urbanisme).	● L'imprimé de demande. ● Quatre plans de situation. ● Quatre plans du terrain.

b) Demande sur les possibilités de réaliser l'opération suivante : (article L. 410.1.b. du Code de l'urbanisme).
 	
● Construction, établissement commercial ou lotissement.
 	
● Installation de caravanes, aménagement d'un terrain de camping ou de caravanage, ou d'un parc résidentiel de loisirs.
● Installations et travaux divers. Association foncière urbaine, autre opération.
	● L'imprimé de demande.
	● Quatre plans de situation.
	● Quatre plans du terrain.
	● Une note descriptive du projet en 4 exemplaires permettant d'apprécier la nature et l'importance de l'opération. Elle peut comprendre des croquis, des photos. Elle précise selon les cas :
	  - Le nombre et la destination des bâtiments, le nombre de logements, les surfaces hors œuvres brutes et nettes des bâtiments à conserver, à démolir, selon leur affectation.
	
	  - L'indication sur les plans des équipements desservant le terrain s'il s'agit d'une opération importante, et le nombre des emplacements.
	
	  - La description de l'opération.

c) Demande de certificat d'urbanisme obligatoire précédant la cession d'un terrain issu d'une propriété bâtie. (article L. 111.5 du Code de l'urbanisme).	● L'imprimé de demande. La rubrique 1.5. doit être complètement remplie, en ce qui concerne le terrain actuel. Toutefois pour les terrains agricoles très vastes et qui ne supportent que de petites constructions, il suffit d'indiquer la surface hors œuvre brute approximative des bâtiments. ● Quatre plans de situation. ● Quatre plans du terrain : lorsque le demandeur souhaite connaître la répartition de la surface hors œuvre nette sur chacun des terrains issus de la division, il indique la ligne de partage de la division projetée, la surface des terrains issus de la division (A, B, C...), la(ou les) surfaces(s) hors œuvre(s) nette(s) du(ou des) bâtiment(s) existant(s).
d) Demande de certificat d'urbanisme obligatoire exigé avant toute division du terrain en vue de la construction et non soumise à la réglementation des lotissements. (article R. 315.54 du Code de l'urbanisme).	● L'imprimé de demande. La rubrique a.5. doit être complètement remplie. ● Quatre plans de situation. ● Quatre plans du terrain faisant apparaître obligatoirement les limites des lots, leur superficie, leur dénomination (A, B, C...). La (ou les) surface(s) hors œuvre(s) nette(s) du(ou des) bâtiment(s) existant(s), leur affectation.

AM 390 ⚓ 22-01-59 **sofiac** édition. tél. 02 35 77 41 41 - B.P. 145, 76410 saint-aubin-lès-elbeuf (9706)

168

A VOTRE CHOIX, VOUS POUVEZ :

● ENVOYER VOTRE DEMANDE PAR LA POSTE :

Vous adressez au Maire de la commune où se situe le terrain, par pli recommandé, avec demande d'avis de réception postal :

— l'imprimé de demande dont vous conservez le dernier feuillet,
— quatre plans de situation,
— quatre plans du terrain,
— le cas échéant, une notice descriptive du projet en quatre exemplaires.

● DÉPOSER VOTRE DEMANDE A LA MAIRIE (de la commune où se situe le terrain) :

Vous remettez : — l'imprimé de demande,
— quatre plans de situation,
— quatre plans du terrain,
— le cas échéant, une notice descriptive du projet en quatre exemplaires.

Il vous est rendu le dernier feuillet de l'imprimé de demande après signature du récépissé de dépôt.

Des exemplaires supplémentaires de l'imprimé de demande et du dossier pourront vous être demandés pour les services, personnes publiques ou commissions consultés sur la demande.

3 – DÉLIVRANCE DU CERTIFICAT D'URBANISME

Le certificat d'urbanisme est délivré, selon les cas, par le Maire, le Président de l'Établissement Public de Coopération Inter-communale auquel le Maire aurait éventuellement délégué sa compétence, ou par le Préfet après observations du Maire. Il est délivré dans un délai de deux mois. Il est valable pendant un an au minimum.

4 – INFORMATION IMPORTANTE

Le certificat d'urbanisme a pour objet de faire connaître au demandeur les seules limitations **administratives** au droit de propriété concernant le terrain ou le projet ainsi que la desserte de celui-ci par les équipements publics existants ou prévus.

Il appartient donc au demandeur de s'assurer, indépendamment de sa demande de certificat d'urbanisme et préalablement à tout projet, que celui-ci respecte bien les **droits privés des tiers intéressés** (propriétaire du sol, copropriétaires, voisins, ...), notamment par l'examen des servitudes ou obligations mentionnées sur les titres de propriété ou les baux. A défaut, sa responsabilité risquerait d'être engagée, même dans le cas où un certificat d'urbanisme positif lui serait par ailleurs délivré.

La loi n° 78-17 du 6 janvier 1978 relative à l'informatique, aux fichiers et aux libertés s'applique aux réponses faites à ce formulaire par les personnes physiques. Elle garantit un droit d'accès et de rectification pour les données vous concernant auprès de la Mairie ou de la Direction Départementale de l'Equipement.

N° 10543*01

MINISTÈRE DE L'ÉQUIPEMENT,
DES TRANSPORTS ET DU LOGEMENT

DEMANDE DE CERTIFICAT D'URBANISME

C U				

Cadre réservé à l'administration

Dép¹	Commune	Année	Numéro du dossier

● 1 - TERRAIN (1)

1 - 1 - ADRESSE DU TERRAIN 4 RUE VOLTAIRE 34300 AGDE

1 - 2 - NOM ET ADRESSE DU PROPRIÉTAIRE (s'il n'est pas le demandeur)

1 - 3 - CADASTRE : Section(s) cadastrale(s) et pour chaque section, numéro des parcelles.

1 - 4 - ORIGINE
Si un certificat d'urbanisme a déjà été délivré pour le terrain,

NUMÉRO du certificat . . . . | _ _ | _ _ _ | _ _ |

Le terrain est-il situé dans un lotissement : | OUI | NON | ne sait pas |
NUMÉRO du(des) lot(s) . . . . :
. . . . :
Lotissement autorisé le
NOM du lotissement ou du lotisseur :
S'agit-il d'un terrain ISSU depuis moins de 10 ans d'une plus grande
propriété ? . . . . : | OUI | NON |

1 - 5 - SUPERFICIE ET OCCUPATION ACTUELLE (2)

	Terrain désigné en 1-3·	en cas de division projetée (objet c et d de la demande)			
		Terrain A	Terrain B	Terrain C	Terrain D
Surface du terrain (en m2)	808m²				
S.H.O.B. (3) des constructions existantes (en m2)					
S.H.O.N. (4) des constructions existantes (en m2)					
Affectation des constructions existantes (logements, commerces...)					
Date d'édification des constructions en cas de C.U. c) (cf. rubrique 3)					

Le terrain est-il boisé ? . . . . : | OUI | NON |
Nature et importance du boisement . . . :

● 2 - DEMANDEUR

NOM - PRÉNOM (ou raison sociale)

SMITH, JOHN

ADRESSE 6 GLEBE CLOSE WORTHING, SUSSEX ANGLETERRE

● 3 - OBJET DE LA DEMANDE
La demande de certificat d'urbanisme peut porter sur plusieurs objets.

a. ☐ Demande en vue de savoir si le terrain est constructible ou non (L. 410.1.a. du Code de l'Urbanisme).

b. ☐ Demande sur les possibilités de réaliser l'opération suivante (L. 410.1.b. du Code de l'Urbanisme) :
 ○ Construction à usage de :
 ○ Lotissement
 ○ Stationnement d'une à six caravanes pendant plus de 3 mois
 ○ Aménagement d'un terrain de camping ou de caravanage
 ○ Aménagement d'un parc résidentiel de loisirs
 ○ Installations et travaux divers :
  ☐ Parc d'attractions ou aire de jeux et de sport ouvert au public
  ☐ Aire de stationnement ouverte au public } susceptible de contenir au moins dix unités
  ☐ Dépôt de véhicules
  ☐ Garage collectif de caravanes
  ☐ Affouillement du sol } de plus de 100 m² de surface et de plus de 2 m de
  ☐ Exhaussement du sol } profondeur ou de hauteur
 ○ Association foncière urbaine
 ○ Autre opération ; nature :

c. ☐ Demande de certificat d'urbanisme obligatoire précédant la cession d'un terrain issu d'une propriété bâtie (L. 111.5 du Code de l'urbanisme).
Sanction : nullité de la vente en cas d'absence de certificat.

d. ☐ Demande de certificat d'urbanisme obligatoire exigé avant toute division non soumise à la réglementation des lotissements (R. 315.54 du Code de l'urbanisme).
Sanction : amende en cas d'absence de certificat.

● 4 - ENGAGEMENT DU DEMANDEUR

Je certifie exacts les renseignements mentionnés dans les rubriques ci-dessus (5)

Date et signature

Lib Smith   30 JUIN 1999

---

(1) **TERRAIN** : Le terrain est l'îlot de propriété constitué par la parcelle ou par l'ensemble des parcelles contiguës appartenant à un même propriétaire ou à une même indivision.

(2) Les renseignements que vous ne pouvez pas indiquer à la rubrique 1.5. seront repris dans une NOTE DESCRIPTIVE.

(3) **La surface hors œuvre BRUTE (S.H.O.B.) des constructions** est égale à la somme des surfaces de plancher de chaque niveau de ces constructions, calculée à partir de l'extérieur des murs de façades, y compris les balcons, les loggias, les toitures-terrasses, les combles et les sous-sols aménageables ou non (article R.112-2 du Code de l'Urbanisme).

(4) **La surface hors œuvre NETTE (S.H.O.N.) des constructions** est égale à la surface hors œuvre brute de ces constructions après déduction des surfaces de plancher hors œuvre :
 a) des combles et des sous-sols non aménageables pour l'habitation ou pour des activités à caractère professionnel, artisanal, industriel ou commercial : locaux ou parties de locaux d'une hauteur inférieure à 1,80 mètre (calculée à partir de la face interne de la toiture ou du plafond) ou constituant des locaux techniques (chaufferies, machineries d'ascenseurs...) ou caves ;
 b) des toitures-terrasses, des balcons, des loggias, ainsi que des surfaces non closes situées au rez-de-chaussée ;
 c) des bâtiments ou des parties de bâtiments aménagées en vue du stationnement des véhicules ;
 d) des bâtiments affectés au logement des récoltes, des animaux ou du matériel agricole ainsi que des surfaces des serres de production ;
 e) d'une surface égale à 5 pour 100 des surfaces hors œuvre affectées à l'habitation telles qu'elles résultent, le cas échéant, des déductions prévues aux a. b et c ci-dessus.

Sont également déduites de la surface hors œuvre, dans le cas de la réfection d'un immeuble à usage d'habitation et dans la limite de cinq mètres carrés par logement les surfaces de planchers affectées à la réalisation de travaux tendant à l'amélioration de l'hygiène des locaux et celles résultant de la fermeture de balcons, loggias et surfaces non closes situées en rez-de-chaussée.

RÉCEPTION DE LA DEMANDE
La présente demande a été reçue ce jour en Mairie.
Fait à :
Le :

(5) Les inexactitudes éventuelles qui figurent dans les rubriques engagent la responsabilité du demandeur si elles entraînent des préjudices ou des inexactitudes dans la réponse. Elles peuvent entacher de nullité le certificat.

AM 390 ☎ 22-01-59 sofiac édition, tel 02 35 77 41 41 - B.P. 145, 76410 saint-aubin-lès-elbeuf (9706)

APPLICATION FOR TOWN PLANNING

No. 10543*01

Answer questions on the form using a typewriter or black biro.
Write on the top copy only
Press firmly on a hard surface.

1 – TO BE INCLUDED WITH APPLICATION

1 – 1   The dossier must include:

- *CERTIFICATE 10543*01 DULY COMPLETED* [top copy only]

- *FOUR COPIES OF AN AREA MAP*:
  Scale between 1/5000 and 1/25000, on paper format 21 x 29.7 [A4 size]
  showing:
    - The orientation [i.e. north, south, etc.];
    - Local roads and their classification;
    - Landmarks and references to pinpoint your property.

The above are obtainable at your local Mairie, Department of Urbanisme.

- *A PLAN OF YOUR LAND OR PROPERTY*:
  Scale between 1/500 and 1/5000, if possible on A4 paper showing:
    - Boundary dimensions:
    - Access roads;
    - Position of existing buildings.

- *A BRIEF DESCRIPTION OF PLANNED ALTERATIONS OF BUILDINGS*

1 – 2   A permit will be required for any of following four reasons, so the application will vary according to each individual case. However, you should still use just the one form [10543*01] for multi-purpose applications.

PURPOSE OF APPLICATION	TO BE INCLUDED WITH APPLICATION
a) To ascertain if planning permission will be granted on your land	• Form 10543*01. • Four plans of existing building. • Four area maps.
b) What you propose to build or change.	• Form 10543*01. • Four plans of existing buildings and land. • Four area maps. • Four descriptions of proposals showing dimensions and including sketches and/or photos. These must show:

171

• Buildings, commercial or residential	— The number and use of buildings, buildings, amount of accommodation, surface areas (gross and net, i.e. internal and external) to conserve or demolish, etc.
• Installation of caravans, a camping site or leisure park	— An indication of planned use of land and number of sites, plus toilet and shower buildings, etc.
• Installation of industrial works or other operations	— Description of operation
c) Application for obligatory planning certificate preceding the assigning of the land.	• Form 10543*01 with section 1.5 fully completed. In the case of large areas of agricultural land with only a few small buildings it is sufficient to indicate the approximate external area of the buildings. • Four plans of proposals. • Four land plans [maps]: when the land is to be subdivided into separate plots, the divisions are to be indicated plus the area of each plot (A, B, C, etc.) and positions of existing buildings.
d) Application for obligatory planning certificate before dividing up land for sale, bearing in mind that anything over two plots becomes an estate – lotissement – thus different regulations apply.	• Form 10543*01 with section 5 fully completed. • Four area maps. • Four plans of the land showing boundaries and surface area of each plot (which should be marked A, B, C, etc.) plus any existing buildings showing both internal and external dimensions.

2 – DEPOSITING YOUR APPLICATION

YOU MAY, IF YOU CHOOSE:

• SEND YOUR APPLICATION BY POST:

It should be addressed to the Mairie where the land or house is sited and sent by registered post with a request for notification of receipt.

You should enclose, as already stated, the four area maps and four site plans plus a description of the plans. Keep the bottom copy of form 10543*01.

- TAKE YOUR APPLICATION BY HAND TO THE MAIRIE:

> You should enclose, as already stated, the four area maps and four site plans plus a description of the plans.
>
> He will sign and stamp the bottom copy of form 10543*01 and hand it back to you.

3 – DELIVERY OF THE PLANNING APPROVAL

The certificate will be sent to you by the Mairie (in most cases) within two months. It is valid for at least a year.

4 – IMPORTANT INFORMATION

Planning approval is issued if the application is in accordance with local or national administrative regulations.

It is up to the applicant to make sure that the plans will in no way affect neighbours or co-proprietors (in the case of apartments) or land owners (in the case of rented property).

Note
The example shown of the completed form 10543*01 will be all that is normally necessary in most cases, i.e. a privately owned house or land which will not need to be divided up into lots.

Glossary

French – English

Abîmer	Spoil, damage, deteriorate
Abonnement	Standing charge
Abri	Shed, shelter
Acajou	Mahogany
Accrochage	Hanging up, fixing
Accueil	Reception
Agence immobilier	Estate Agency
Agglomere	Chipboard
Alimentation	Feed, supply (water, electricity etc.)
Ampoule	Light bulb
Antenne	Aerial
Antibélier	Expansion chamber to absorb plumbing vibration
Appartement	Apartment, flat
Arbre	Tree
Ardoise	Slate tile
Armoire	Cabinet (bathroom etc.)
Arrêt de façade	Shutter fastening
Arrosage	Watering (garden etc.)
Arroseur	Sprinkler
Artisan Carreleur	Ceramic tiling expert
Artisan Maçon	Builder
Aspirateur	Vacuum cleaner
Atelier	Workshop
Auge	Mixing trough
Avocat	Solicitor
Bâche	Tarpaulin
Baguette	Trim, beading etc.
Baignoire	Bath
Balai	Broom
Bâtiment	Building
Bêche	Spade
Béton	Concrete

174

Bétonnière	Concrete mixer
Bicône	Compression joint (with olives)
Bois	Wood
Boîte à Onglets	Mitre box
Bouche d'Aeration	Air vent
Bouchon	Stopper, blanking cap, etc.
Boulon	Bolt
Brouette	Wheelbarrow
Cabinet WC	Toilet
Cadenas	Padlock
Cadre	Frame
Calcaire	Calcium
Cale	Wedge
Caoutchouc	Rubber
Carillon	Door bell
Carrelage	Ceramic tiles
Catalyst	Catalyseur
Charnière	Hinge
Charpentier	Carpenter
Château	Castle, large country house
Chaudière	boiler
Chauffe-eau	Hot water tank
Chaume	Thatch
Chaux	Carbonate of lime
Cheminée	Fireplace and chimney
Chêne	Oak
Cheville	Expanding wall plug (Rawlplug)
Ciment	Cement
Cisailles	Shears
Ciseau à bois	Wood chisel
Ciseau de briqueteur	Brick chisel, cold chisel
Clef	Spanner
Clef à Molette	Adjustable spanner
Climatisation	Air conditioning
Cloison	Partition
Clôture	Fence
Clou	Nail
Colle	Glue
Collet batu	Flanged copper pipe plus nut for fibre washer
Compromis de vente	Sale agreement
Congélateur	Freezer
Contre-plaqué	Plywood

Corniche	Coving
Coude	Bend (as in plumbing)
Coulisse	slide (drawer slide etc.)
Coupe carreaux	tile cutter
Cremone	Rotating handle on shutters and windows
Crépi	Stucco, rough coating
Croisillons	Trellis or ceramic tile separators
Crochet	Catch (door catch etc.)
Cuisine	Kitchen
Cuisinière	Cooker
Cuivre	Copper
Cuvette	Toilet pan
Dallage	Paving
Dalle	Flag stone, paving stone, quarry tile
Décapent	Scourer, paint stripper
Décharge public	Local tip
Découpage	Cutting to size or to order
Défonceuses	Router
Dépôt de vente	Sale-room
Détendeur	Gas pressure regulator
Devis	Estimate
Disjoncteur	Trip switch, circuit breaker
Domino	Plastic electric strip connectors
Douche	Shower
Douchette	Shower rose
Eau de javel	Bleach
Ebénist	Cabinet maker
Echafaudage	Scaffolding
Échelle	Ladder
Éclairage	Lighting
Écrous	Nut
Electrode	Welding rod
Encadrement	Framing
Enduit	Filler
Entretien	Upkeep, maintenance
Épaisseur	Thickness
Équerre	Set square
Escabeau	Step ladder
Escalier	Staircase
Espagnolette	Shutter or window fastening
Établi	Work bench

Étagère	Shelves
Étais de maçon	Builders' extending props
Étanche	Watertight
Étau	Bench vice
Évier	Kitchen sink
Faîltière	Ridge tile
Fenêtre	Window
Fer	Iron
Ferraillage	Ironwork (rod, joists, etc.)
Ferronnerie	(As above)
Fers à Souder	Soldering iron
Fibres Dures	Hardboard
Fil à Plomb	Plumb line
Fondation	Foundation
Fongicide	Fungicide
Forêt	Drill bit
Fosse Septique	Septic tank
Foyer	Fireplace
Frigo	Fridge
Gaine	Sheathing (electrical conduit, etc.)
Garde-corps	Railings
Gazon	Turf
Gond	Shutter hinge pin
Gouttière	Gutter
Grange	Barn
Grattoir	Scraper
Gravier	Gravel
Grenier	Loft
Griffe	Tile scorer
Grillage	Wire mesh, netting, fencing
Grille	Gate, iron grill over window
Groupe électrogènes	Generator
Groupe de sécurité	safety valve
Haie	Hedge
Huile de lin	Linseed oil
Inox	Stainless steel
Inter horaire	Time switch
Interrupteur	Switch (on/of)
Isolation	Insulation

Jardin	Garden
Joint	Grouting (for ceramic tiles)
Jumelle	Semi-detached house
Laine d'acier	Wire wool
Laiton	Brass
Lambris	Tongued and grooved wood panelling
Lampe à sonder	Blow lamp
Largeur	Width
Latté	Blockboard
Lavabo	Wash basin
Lave-mains	Hand basin
Liège	Cork tiling
Lime	File
Linteau	Lintel
Lisse	Smooth
Location	Hire
Longeur	Length
Loqueteau	Door catch
Lucarne	Dormer window
Maçon	Builder
Maillet	Mallet
Maire	Mayor
Mairie	Town Hall
Maison	House
Maisonette	Cottage
Maison jumelle	Semi detached house
Manchon	Straight coupling (plumbing joint)
Manchon reduit	Reduction joint
Marquise	Porch
Marteau	Hammer
Marteau de démolition	Mechanical hammer
Mazout	Home heating oil
Mèche	Drill bit
Menuiserie	Woodwork factory or warehouse
Meubles	Furniture
Meuleuse	Angle grinder
Minuterie	Timer
Miroir	Mirror
Mitoyenne	Party wall
Mortier	Mortar
Mortier Colle	Tile cement

French	English
Moquette	Fitted carpet
Moulure	Moulding
Mur	Wall
Nettoyant	Cleaning fluid
Notaire	Notary
Paillasson	Door mat
Panne	Breakdown (en panne – broken down)
Panneau	Panel
Papier Peint	Wall paper
Parquet	Wood flooring
Peinture	Paint
Pelle	Shovel
Pelouse	Lawn
Pépinière	Garden centre
Perceuse	Drill
Petites Annonces	Small advertisements
Pièce	Room (kitchen & bathroom not counted)
Pierre	Stone
Pilier	Pillar
Pin	Pine
Pinceau	Paint Brush
Pince universal	Pliers
Pipe à sortie	Evacuation pipe
Piquet de Terre	Earthing pin
Placard	Cupboard
Plafond	Ceiling
Planche	Plank
Plancher	Floor
Plâtre	Plaster
Plomberie	Plumbing
Poignée	Handle
Pompe	Pump
Ponceuse	Orbital sander
Ponceuse à bande	Belt sander
Portail	Garden gate
Porte (bloc porte)	Door (plus frame)
Porte coulissante	Sliding door
Poste de soudage à l'arc	Arc welder
Poteaux	Post
Poussière	Dust

Poutre	Beam
Poutre apparente	Exposed beam
Poutre en fer	Girder, RSJ (rigid steel joist)
Poutrelle	Small beam
Prise	Electric socket
Prise de terre	Earthing point
Produit	Product
Programmateur	Programmer
Prolongateur	Extension lead
Promesse de vente	A promise to sell
Quincaillerie	Hardware shop
Rabot	Plane
Raccord	Connection
Radiateur soufflant	Fan heater
Ragréage	Self-levelling screed
Ramoneur	Chimney-sweep
Râteau	Rake
Reçu	Receipt
Regard de visite	Inspection chamber
Régle niveau	Spirit level
Remise	Garage/store
Réservoir	Cistern
Revêtement	New facing or coating
Rideau	Curtain
Rive de toit	Roof edge
Robinet	Tap
Robinet purgeur	Drain-off cock
Roche	Rock
Rondelle	Washer
Rosace	Ceiling rose
Rouleau	Roller (paint roller)
Sable	Sand
Sapin	Fir
Scie	Saw
Scie Circulaire	Circular saw
Scie à meteaux	Hack saw
Scie à Ruban	Band saw
Scie sauteuse	Jig saw
Scie vilebrequin	Ceramic tile cutting saw
Seau	Bucket
Séjour (salle de)	Living-room

Serre-joint	Clamp (G clamp etc.)
Serrure	Lock
Service d'eau	Water authority
Siphon	water trap (U bend etc.)
Sol	Ground (re. tiles etc.)
Soudure	Solder
Sous couche	Undercoat
Store	Roller blind
Store Vénitiens	Venetian blind
Taloche	Plasterers float
Tamis	Sieve
Tapis	Carpet, rug
Tartre	Lime deposit
Teck	Teak
Terre cuite	Terracotta, unglazed brick or tile
Terrasse	Terrace
Terre	Earth
Textile muraux	Fabric wall coverings
Tiroir	Drawer
Tissu	Cloth, fabric
Toit	Roof
Tondeuse	Lawn mower
Touret	Beach grinder
Tournevis	Screwdriver
Treillis soudés	Welded steel mesh
Tréteau	Trestle
Tronçonneuse	Chain saw
Truelle	Trowel
Tuile	Roof tile
Tuile de rive	Edge tile
Tuyau	Tube, pipe (hosepipe etc.)
Vanne	Gate valve, heavy duty tap
Variateur	Dimmer switch
Vernis	Varnish
Vitre	Glass
Villa	Detached house
Vis	Screw
Volet	Shutter
Volige	Thin plank

Glossary

English – French

Adjustable spanner	Clef à Molette
Advice	Conseil
Aerial	Antenne
Air conditioning	Climatization
Air vent	Bouche d'aeration
Angle grinder	Meuleuse
Arc welder	Poste de soudage à l'arc
Assembly	Montage
Bandsaw	Scie à ruban
Barn	Grange
Bath	Bagnoire
Beading	Baguette
Beam	Poutre
Belt sander	Penceuse a bande
Bench vice	Etau
Bend (plumbing)	Coude
Blockboard	Latté
Blow lamp	Lampe à sonder
Boiler	Chaudière
Bolt	Boulon
Brakedown	Panne
Brass	Laiton
Brick	Brique
Brick chisel	Ciseau de briqueteur
Broom	Balai
Bucket	Seau
Builder	Maçon
Builder's props (acrow)	Étais de maçon
Building	Bâtiment
Cabinet	Armoire
Cabinet maker	Ébéniste
Carpet	Tapis
Catch (door/cupboard)	Crochet

Ceiling	Plafond
Ceiling rose	Rosace
Cement	Ciment
Chainsaw	Tronçonneuse
Chimney	Cheminée
Chimney sweep	Ramoneur
Chipboard	Agglomérés
Cistern	Reservoir
Clamp (G clamp etc)	Serre joint
Cleaner (fluid)	Nettoyant
Cloth (fabric etc.)	Tissu
Compression joint	Bicône
Concrete	Béton
Concrete mixer	Bétonnière
Conduit (electrical)	Gaine
Connection	Raccord
Copper	Cuivre
Coving	Corniche
Circuit breaker	Disjoncteur
Cupboard	Placard
Curtain	Rideau
Cutting to order (wood etc.)	Découpage
Deteriorate	Abimer
Dimmer switch	Variateur
Door	Porte
Doorbell	Carillon
Door catch	Loqueteau/crochet
Doormat	Paillasson
Dormer window	Lucarne
Drain off cock	Robinet de purgeur
Drawer	Tiroir
Drill	Perceuse
Drill bit	Forêt/Mèche
Dust	Poussière
Earth	Terre
Earth (electrical)	Prise de Terre
Earthing pin/strap	Piquet de terre
Edge of roof	Rive de toit
Edge roof tile	Tuile de rive
Electrical strip connectors	Domino

Estate agency	Agence immobilier
Estimate	Devis
Evacuation pipe	Pipe à sortie
Expanding plug (wall fixing)	Cheville
Exposed beam	Poutre Apparente
Extension lead	Prolongateur
Extractor fan	Aerateur
Fabric wall coverings	Textile muraux
Facing (coating etc.)	Revêtement
Fan	Ventilateur
Fan heater	Radiateur soufflant
Feed (of water, electricity)	Alimentation
Fence	Clôture
Fencing (mesh, chain link)	Grillage
File	Lime
Filler	Enduit/reboucheur
Fir/pine	Sapin
Fire place	Cheminée
Fitted carpet	Moquette
Flag stone (quarry tile etc.)	Dalle
Foundation	Fondation
Frame	Cadre
Framing	Encadrement
Fungicide	Fongicide
Furniture	Meubles
Garden	Jardin
Gate	Grille/Portrail
Gate valve (heavy duty tap)	Vanne
Generator	Groupe électrogènes
Girder (RSJ)	Poutre en fer
Glass (window type)	Vitre
Glue	Colle
Gravel	Gravier
Grout (for ceramic tiles)	Joint
Gutter	Gouttière
Hacksaw	Scie à meteaux
Hammer	Marteau
Handle	Poignée
Hanging fixing	Accrochage
Hardboard	Fibres cure – Issorelle
Hedge	Haie
Hinge	Charnière

Hire	Location
Hotwater Tank	Chauffe-eau
House	Maison
Inspection chamber	Regarde de visite
Insulation	Isolation
Iron	Fer
Ironwork	Ferronerie
Jigsaw	Scie sauteuse
Joint (straight coupling)	Manchon
Joint reduction	Manchon Reduit
Key	Clé
Kitchen	Cuisine
Ladder	Échelle
Lawn	Pelouse
Lawnmower	Tendeuse
Length	Longeur
Light bulb	Ampoule
Lighting	Éclairage
Lime (carbonate of)	Chaux
Linseed oil	Huile de Lin
Lintel	Linteau
Living-room	Séjour (salle de)
Lock	Serrure
Mahogany	Acajou
Maintenance	Entretien
Mallet	Maillet
Mechanical hammer	Marteau de démolition
Mesh (wire)	Grillage
Mirror	Miroir
Mitre box	Bôite à onglets
Mixing trough	Auge
Mortar	Mortier
Moulding	Moulure
Nail	Clou
Notary (conveyancing lawyer)	Notaire
Nut	Écrou
Oak	Chêne
Oil	Mazout

Orbital sander	Ponceuse
Padlock	Cadenas
Paint	Peinture
Paint brush	Pinceau
Paint roller	Rouleau à peindre
Panel	Panneau
Panelling (wood strip/ tongue & groove etc.)	Lambris
Partition	Cloison
Party wall	Mitoyenne
Paving	Dallage
Pillar	Pilier
Pine	Sapin
Pipe	Pipe – tuyau
Plank	Planche
Plaster	Plâtre
Pliers	Pince universal
Plumb line	Fil à plomb
Plywood	Contre-plaqué
Product	Produit
Programmer	Programmateur
Porch	Marquise
Post (fencing)	Poteaux
Pump	Pompe
Rafter	Chevron
Rake	Râteau
Regulator (gas)	Détendeur
Ridge tile	Faîtière
Rodding eye	Tampon visite
Roller blind	Store
Roof	Toit
Router	Defonceuses
Sand	Sable
Sand Merchant	Sablier
Saw	Scie
Scaffolding	Echafaudage
Scraper	Grattoir
Screw	Vis
Screwdriver	Tournevis
Self levelling screed	Ragreage
Semi-detached house	Jumelle
Septic tank	Fosse septique

Sieve	Tamis
Set square	Équerre
Shears	Cisailles
Shed	Abri
Shelf	Étagère
Shovel	Pelle
Shower	Douche
Shower rose	Douchette
Shower basin	Bac à douche - receveur
Shutter	Volet
Shutter fastening	Espagnolette
Shutter hinge pin	Gond
Sink (kitchen)	Évier
Slate (tile)	Ardoise
Slide (for drawer)	Coulisse
Sliding door	Port coulissant
Smooth	Lisse
Soap	Savon
Soap holder	Porte savon
Socket (electric)	Prise
Solder	Soudure
Soldering iron	Fers à souder
Spade	Bêche
Spanner	Clef
Spirit level	Régle niveau
Sprinkler	Arroseur
Staircase	Escalier
Stainless steel	Inox
Step ladder	Escabeau
Stone	Pierre
Straight coupling (plumbing)	Manchon
Stucco	Crépi
Switch	Interupteur
Tap	Robinet
Tarpaulin	Bâche
Teak	Teck
Terra Cotta	Terre cuite
Terrace	Terrasse
Thatch	Chaume
Thickness	Épaisseur
Tiles (roof)	Tuiles
Tiles (ceramic)	Carrelage
Tile grout	Joint carrelage

Tile cutter	Coupe carrelage
Tile cement	Mortier colle etc.
Tile scorer	Griffe
Time switch	Inter horaire
Timer	Minuterie
Toilet pan	Cuvette
Towel rail	Porte serviette
Tree	Arbre
Trellis	Croisillons
Trestle	Tréteau
Trowel	Truelle
Turf	Gazon
U bend (water trap)	Siphon
Undercoat	Sous couche
Urinal	Urinoir
Vacuum cleaner	Aspirateur
Varnish	Vernis
Venetian blind	Store Venitien
Wall	Mur
Wallpaper	Papier peint
Wash basin	Lavabo
Wash hand basin	Lave mains
Washer	Rondelle
Water heater	Chaudiere
Water supply	Alimentation d'eau
Watering (garden)	Arrosage
Watertight	Etanche
Wedge	Cale
Welding rod	Electrode
Welder (arc)	Poste de soudage à l'arc
Wheelbarrow	Brouette
Width	Largeur
Window	Fenêtre
Wire mesh or netting	Grillage
Wire wool	Laine d'acier
Wood	Bois
Wood chisel	Ciseau à bois
Wood flooring	Parquet
Woodworking factory	Menuiserie
Work bench	Établi
Workshop	Atelier

Index